SEEKING
THE
SPIRIT

SEEKING
THE How to Create a Community of Seekers
SPIRIT

Harry Brunett and Jennifer Grow

MOREHOUSE PUBLISHING
HARRISBURG / PENNSYLVANIA

Morehouse Publishing, P.O. Box 1321, Harrisburg, PA 17105
Morehouse Publishing, 445 Fifth Avenue, New York, NY 10016
Morehouse Publishing is an imprint of Church Publishing Incorporated.

Cover image: "Quiet Forest," © Royalty-Free/Corbis
Cover design: Lee Singer
Page design: Beth Oberholtzer

Library of Congress Cataloging-in-Publication Data

Brunett, Harry.
    Seeking the Spirit : how to create a community of seekers / Harry Brunett and Jennifer Grow.
        p.   cm.
    Includes bibliographical references.
    ISBN-13: 978-0-8192-2194-0 (pbk.)
    1. Journeys Community (Church : Columbia, Md.) 2. Non-institutional churches—Maryland—Columbia—Case studies. I. Grow, Jennifer. II. Title.
BV601.9.B78   2006
277.3'083—dc22
                                                            2005032116

Printed in the United States of America

06 07 08 09   10 9 8 7 6 5 4 3 2 1

CONTENTS

ACKNOWLEDGMENTS

We would like to express our appreciation and thanks to the following for participating in Journeys Community and for sharing their stories and lending their support and encouragement:

Barbara and Bob Allen; Valerie Bornemann; Marcia Brooks; Joan Brunett; Ken Conklin; Michele and Joe Cosentini; Janis and Jerry Cripe; Kelly Denton-Borhaug; Chuck Donofrio; Emmanuel Episcopal Church; Episcopal Diocese of Maryland; Sally Farrell; Nancy Fitzgerald; Steve Frantz; John and Charlotte Godfrey; Patty Hammer; Tom Hartigan; Barbara Salzman Hastings; Rick and Margaret LaRocca; Dave Leoni; Harry Leffmann; Alison Matusky; Laura Mueller; Jeff, Allyson, and Larisa Nugent; Old St. Paul's Episcopal Church; Patty Pinto; Michael Prowda; Paul Shoffeitt; Mike Smith; Tatiana; Evelyn Templeman; Vaughan Brown Charitable Trust; and all the spiritual seekers at Journeys Community.

FOREWORD

We live in a world of "seekers." Most of us are seeking the things that truly give life meaning, things that will help us reach our highest potential and contribute to lasting joy and a sense of fulfillment. People inside the church are seeking these same things no less—or more—than people outside. All of us are on a similar journey.

For centuries—in Christianity as well as in many other faith traditions—the journey has been used as an analogy for spiritual growth and development. It's easy to see why: as with a physical journey, the spiritual journey unfolds before us, taking many different paths, bringing us a variety of experiences along the way, and bringing us to a destination that's a mystery to us when we set out. All of us are on a journey in which God and our companion human beings intersect our path, influencing the directions we choose, the paths we take, and what we learn along the way.

So when church people assume our sole task is to walk the journey, sharing our faith with others, encouraging them to become like us, we quickly discover it's never quite that simple. Polls indicate that the vast majority of Americans believe in God and value spirituality. But in increasing numbers, people of all ages don't identify themselves with any particular religious group. So if we're going to journey together, Christians will have to learn better ways to communicate, better ways to truly listen to our neighbors outside the church. The old attitude, "We have the goods, so sit at our feet and learn from us" (though never stated so crassly), simply doesn't work. There's too much mistrust. Moreover, the presumption that "we have the goods" isn't an accurate description of the work of the Holy Spirit in a world in which people experience God in many different ways.

In my own journey I continue to be informed—and my faith continues to be strengthened—by both the witness of those inside the church and the witness of others who have no church experience. God works in and through people and isn't constrained to just one faith tradition or one religious experience. We as Christians need to balance our desire to share the good news of Jesus Christ in our world with our need to love and honor our neighbors enough to respect their journeys and anticipate that the Holy Spirit may be working in them as well. That is, we need to be in dialogue—not monologue—and we need to find ways to journey together.

For those of us who have found faith communities to be places of spiritual nourishment and personal support, there are new challenges when it comes to creating meaningful approaches to a relationship with God. Over the past several years, Journeys Community, described in this book, has attempted to engage persons outside the church in meaningful dialogue. Its purpose has been to identify seekers' needs and aspirations, provide them with community and support, and enable them to pursue their own spiritual paths. In a sense, Journeys Community has been a pilot project exploring more appropriate ways for church communities and others to engage and affirm seekers in the world.

I'm pleased that the Episcopal Diocese of Maryland has from the beginning of this project been a sponsor. The initial leaders of Journeys Community were Episcopalians. The Episcopal Church has a long tradition of openness to diverse opinions and acceptance of theological differences within the community of faith. Yet the insights gleaned from this project will benefit more than just Episcopalians. I applaud this fine work and have the greatest respect for the men and women who've produced Journeys Community as a labor of love and a gift to all God's people.

The Right Reverend Robert W. Ihloff, D.Min., D.D.
Bishop of Maryland

PREFACE

There are many religious people worldwide who are inspiring examples of what it means to live compassionately. They're willing to love, serve, and accept others without judgment. We appreciate the goodness these people contribute through their attitudes and actions. It's important to acknowledge at the beginning of this book that traditional religion has worked—and continues to work—for millions of people, bringing them into a closer relationship with God and with other human beings.

But just as religion serves millions of people and brings them in contact with the Divine, there are also millions whom the church fails to serve. At Journeys Community, we think it's important to represent the views of spiritual seekers for whom religion hasn't worked. This book is written for those people who feel they've been overlooked, unrepresented, or unserved by traditional religion. We know there are people like us who want to deepen their connection to the Divine but have found religion to be either irrelevant in their lives, too laden with dogma, or too limiting in its view. Many of us at one time or another have been regular church members but have come to regard the traditional church as intolerant of our need to seek God in less conventional ways.

The occasional unfavorable representation of religion in this book isn't meant to be a criticism of all religions. Nor is it meant to convince people who are already well served by religion to change their spiritual paths. But it's important to acknowledge the perspective of millions of people who are uninterested in church, or who have resentments against the church that may keep them from a deeper spiritual life. We wish to reflect the opinions and experience of those spiritual seekers who fail to see the relevance of religious practice and doctrine in contemporary society, those who have suffered from the effects of church dogma, church politics, intolerance, judgment, and religious exclusivism—and even those who have simply come to disagree with religious beliefs.

When we refer to traditional religion or the traditional church in an unflattering light, we are primarily referring to fundamentalist Christians, whether evangelical or conservative, as well as extremists of other religions who insist that there is only one true path to God. In America, where religion has been hijacked by the extreme right and turned into a political force, the word "fundamentalist" is a catchall term for conservative Christians. As Bruce Bawer notes in *Stealing Jesus*, "Conservative Christians, unlike liberal Christians, tend to define the word 'Christian' in such a way as to exclude others—in most cases, a large number of their fellow conservative Christians."[1] It's unfortunate that religions worldwide have suffered the negative associations of fundamentalism. The peace and goodness that a belief in God can bring into a person's life through religion has been overshadowed by the message of exclusivism and intolerance that fundamentalism preaches. Unfortunately, the church as a whole has been stigmatized by fundamentalism, preventing it from becoming a viable spiritual path for many seekers.

So the traditional church has turned a blind eye to itself, unable to see itself clearly—unable to see itself as the larger non-churchgoing public sees it. But this book isn't a comprehensive study of the failings or successes of the contemporary church, nor is it meant to analyze ways the contemporary church can reach out to seekers and attract them into traditional congregations. Though this book takes a look at the effects of modernism and postmodernism on spirituality, it's only to point to the changing views of our times.

Our hope is that the church will recognize that it can't possibly serve everyone with its message—nor should it—and acknowledge that all people have the right to live out their spiritual beliefs as they see fit. Many more people are served on their spiritual paths by a mutual attitude of love and acceptance.

The personal stories in this book represent the experiences of many of us as spiritual seekers who have been searching for ways to grow in our connection with the Divine. In describing the process of developing Journeys Community, we offer a model for building a seeker community that is meant to inspire other spiritual seekers and organizations that wish to create a community of their own, where people can worship the God of their understanding without being told what they should believe or how they should experience God in their lives.

The views of this book come from our personal experience. It's a chronicle of our growth and, we hope, an inspiration for seekers everywhere.

CHAPTER 1

WANDERERS WHO ARE NOT LOST

here's a bumper sticker that reads, "Not all who wander are lost," a quote from J. R. R. Tolkien's trilogy *The Lord of the Rings*. This bit of wisdom describes an attitude that many spiritual seekers share: a sense that the wandering is an essential part of the spiritual journey. It's almost a cliché to say it: *life is not about the destination, but about the journey*. The journey and the experience of one's own life are what hold meaning for us. Tolkien's sentiment honors the art of wandering; it's a lighthearted response to the expectations of a more traditional society.

But the phrase also recognizes that the mere act of wandering labels us as "lost." Unfortunately, in this society, the notion that people are lost also implies that they're somehow unknowing, unstable, or irresponsible. In traditional religions—and fundamentalist Christian churches in particular—the word "lost" assumes the need to be found, the need to be saved, the need to be turned in the proper religious direction. Every spiritual seeker can tell you a story—or a hundred stories—about attempts by Christians to save their souls. With alarming frequency, we're forced to defend our choices and methods of searching for our own relationship to the Divine. It's a shame we need to defend our spiritual paths at all!

Some people, of course, have no sense of meaning in their lives and are truly spiritually lost. But to label all people who are not part of organized religion as lost is to misunderstand the lives and aspirations of seekers. We aren't lost or unstable or unknowing. We've just chosen a different path, sometimes taking a long, meandering route through the church before we discovered that it simply didn't serve all our spiritual needs. We don't fit into a tidy demographic—our spiritual wandering cuts across all boundaries, denominations, ages, and races. And we're not anomalies or misfits. In fact, we're the majority of the God-seeking public. Each of us— at some point in our lives—is a seeker.

Different Ways of Finding God

For people who are actively searching for God and meaning in their lives, there seem to be three distinct ways of approaching the journey. There's the way of mainline churches, where members find solace in their faith and have made peace with religion and ritual though they may not believe all of it. They enjoy being part of their tradition and would rather over-look certain disagreeable aspects of dogma to remain in their church as part of a community.

There's also the way of fundamentalists, who require strict adherence to the literal interpretation of Scripture and sacred writing and the prin-ciples of faith to know God and experience redemption and salvation. They believe themselves to be the keepers of religious truth and view any-thing outside their established belief system as wrong.

Then there's the approach of spiritual seekers, who continually remake their spiritual paths to experience the Divine in their own way and in their own time, incorporating everything along the journey. These are the wanderers who aren't lost.

Not surprisingly, fundamentalists are least apt to understand the art of wandering and are most likely to dismiss the spiritual paths of seekers as misguided, invalid, and unworthy. Fundamentalists and conservative Christians believe that God loves only the "saved" as His true children; to them, spiritual seekers are the "unsaved" people of the secular world.

Obviously, there's a pronounced ideological difference between spiri-tual seekers and fundamentalists. A clash between the two occurs when conservative evangelical church members incorrectly assume that their religion will work for everyone as a means of connecting with God. Or when they press their religious beliefs into areas of political and social reform. Some church members, often condescendingly, consider it their duty to set the rest of us on the "right" path to God.

Unfortunately, there is a near total lack of understanding between seekers and fundamentalists. But seekers aren't without fault in this debate. They often fall back on old resentments against the church, citing bad decisions and unfortunate actions the church has taken a disasterous part in over the centuries. Seekers are often happy to recount their negative experiences, disillusionment, and disappointment in the church. But in the midst of resentments, they overlook or disregard the good that it has done—and continues to do.

In a country founded on the principles of religious freedom, there's a conspicuous lack of tolerance on both sides that only accentuates the rift between us and fails to emphasize our shared beliefs. On both sides of the fence, tolerance is a noble spiritual ideal that's difficult to honor. It's easy to forget that many seekers have been served by the church in one way or another, and many churchgoers practice true compassion and tolerance toward others. But fundamentalism or any type of religious extremism that assumes a moral superiority is divisive and intolerant. Narrow thinking doesn't leave room for free will or allow the spiritual freedom to find a path to the God of our own understanding.

Barriers That Keep Seekers from the Traditional Church

Some seekers admit that one of the barriers that keeps them from joining a church or leads them away from congregations is the fear of being judged or excluded. They feel they must clean up their act before going to church. Others are put off by internal church politics that disrupt congregations and keep seekers from becoming—or staying—involved. Some carry a lot of anger in relation to the idea of church. As one seeker, Carolyn, says, "What does religion have to do with my life? The people are so fake, I wouldn't fit in." Her friend J. P. agrees. "Church is full of hate and hypocrisy." He says, "Fundamentalism scares me. It seems like it's crossed the line from Christianity to insanity. I don't want to have anything to do with that kind of hate. I like what Gandhi said: 'God has no religion.' That's what I believe."

Some seekers are put off by the church's lack of relevancy to the contemporary culture. The language, liturgy, and dogma, and even the formality of the church setting, seem outdated and stifling rather than enlightened. Some seekers find church services repressive, irrelevant, and unsupportive. Colleen, a single mom, has frustrations that run deep. "What keeps me away from traditional church are its homogeneous messages, which are not only less than meaningful for me, but they erode the meaning I make of my life. The traditional church maintains antiquated legalisms in marriage and divorce, family planning, birthing children, schooling them, and providing for their financial well-being. I see the church as generating mass misogyny." Sally says it this way: "When I wanted to get remarried, the Catholic Church wouldn't marry me. In fact, the priest had encouraged me to stay married to my previous husband, a man who was not treating me or my daughters well at all. I had no support from the church when I needed it."

The dynamic of belief is another divisive barrier that turns many seekers away. An unquestioning belief that Jesus is the only path to God and to salvation has become a litmus test to determine whether or not one is a Christian. Members of some traditions, afraid that failing to believe the literal truth of Scripture will call their faith into question, are unwilling to read the Bible as history or as metaphor or as a collection of stories and parables. They assume that if you don't believe all of it—or at least most of it—you're not a Christian.

For seekers, the claim of the Christian tradition—or any tradition—to be the exclusive path to God, the only right way of being in relationship with God, is difficult to accept. We find it impossible to believe that the Creator of the universe, would choose to reveal its divine presence in only one religion—to us that seems both suspicious and unlikely. When polled, most people believe there has to be room for other paths to God. In a 2002 survey[1] Americans were asked to respond to the statement, "My religion is the only true religion." Only 17 percent answered affirmatively, while an overwhelming 78 percent did not. That doesn't mean that people are irreligious. Instead, it suggests that people are open to different ways of seeing and believing.

This willingness to see from other points of view can be considered a more worldly and inclusive stance toward spirituality than the church has traditionally maintained, but fundamentalists take a grave view of any move toward secularism. Some even insist that attendance in mainline churches has declined because the church has grown too lenient in accommodating the culture. They believe secularism is dangerous and evil, a corrosive denial of what they believe to be absolute moral truths. In fact, a relative approach to spirituality is in direct conflict with their absolutism—they do not believe that Jesus is one way among many, but that he is the only way. Consider, for example, the best-selling novels in the Left Behind series, coauthored by Tim LaHaye and Jerry Jenkins. They depict Jesus at the second coming, returning to slaughter everyone who isn't a born-again Christian, heaving the world's Hindus, Muslims,

Jews, agnostics—along with many a boatload of Catholics and Unitarians—into an everlasting fire. "Jesus merely raised one hand a few inches and a yawning chasm opened in the earth, stretching far and wide enough to swallow all of them. They tumbled in, howling and screeching."[2] This disturbing image and message—believe or be damned—turns seekers and liberal Christians away from the church in droves. Who wants to believe in a God like that? Yet the aim of the church has been to save sinners and restore people in unity with each other in Christ. There is little room for questioning. Unfortunately, fundamentalism and exclusivism fail to take into account the millions of us for whom traditional religion falls short.

Fundamentalism has also turned seekers away from traditional religion for reasons that are more disturbing. In *The Battle for God*, Karen Armstrong notes:

> Fundamentalists have gunned down worshipers in a mosque, have killed doctors and nurses who work in abortion clinics, have shot their presidents, and have even toppled a powerful government. It is only a small minority of fundamentalists who commit such acts of terror . . . [but they] are perplexing, because they seem so adamantly opposed to many of the most positive values of modern society. Fundamentalists have no time for democracy, pluralism, religious toleration, peacekeeping, free speech, or the separation of church and state. Christian fundamentalists reject the discoveries of biology and physics about the origins of life and insist that the Book of Genesis is scientifically sound in every detail."[3]

There are fundamentalists in every culture and every religion, and they all take an almost perverse comfort in the rigid notion that they are right and therefore "saved" while others are not. Though some people are drawn to extreme beliefs as a means of feeling safe, fundamentalism, as a way of being religious, has turned many others away from the church.

A seeker named Jack is one of them. "Maybe those church people mean well—they want to help us, to save us," he says, "but they don't get it. I don't want to believe what they believe. I'm fine the way I am. I have a God, I pray, I do my own things to worship." Religious people may feel that if unchurched people like Jack truly understood the message of the Gospels, they'd believe. But they fail to grasp that seekers reject the church not because they fail to *understand* the message, but because the message has lost its power to transform their lives.

No wonder the church and the rest of the world are polarized and locked in misunderstanding. Spiritual seekers who have expanded their search for the Divine through more contemporary and postmodern spiritualities are right to take offense. Evangelical fundamentalist Christians have only served to widen the schism between themselves and the secular world. As an unfortunate result, many religions—and Christianity as a whole—have been branded with the uncomely stigma of fundamentalism. Those who have become conservative Christians "out of anger . . . [and] in reaction to spreading secularism," as Bruce Bawer writes in *Stealing Jesus*, have, "in the process, warped Christianity into something ugly and hateful that has little or nothing to do with love and everything to do with suspicion, superstition, and sadism."[4] In fact, the Religious Right has abducted the cultural mode of thought about religion to such an extent that when most Americans hear a person described as "Christian," they come to assume that person is, among other things, intolerant, rigid, judgmental, and mean-spirited. Even liberal and moderate Christians have been made to suffer the stereotype of religious intolerance that the larger society has placed upon them. This doesn't even take into account the negative press the church has received in response to sexual abuse scandals or the issue of gay clergy holding significant church appointments. Christianity is taking a beating. As a religion based on love and compassion as demonstrated by Jesus, Christianity has come to represent something far darker and far more judgmental—at times even hateful—to the larger society. Unfortunately, Christianity has a bad reputation outside the church walls.

Some say that's largely because the church is unable or unwilling to keep pace with the contemporary world. When we suffer a crisis in our lives or begin a spiritual quest, we no longer automatically look to the church for answers. Many seekers feel the church is out of touch with the changes that have taken place in the world and view religion as something archaic, representing a vengeful view of God that's inadequate to deal with people's real concerns. As a result, there has been a crisis of confidence about the Christian tradition. The traditional church isn't keeping pace with society, and its role as the dominant provider of spiritual experience is being challenged. Rather than returning to the institutional church for guidance, many seekers pursue spiritual paths outside the church in nontraditional ways.

So it's completely understandable, if not predictable, that a new spirituality has taken shape over the last few decades in response to the needs of spiritual seekers who have been unable to find meaning in the traditional church.

Wanderers Who Are Not Lost

As spiritual seekers, we know we're not lost. We're merely finding our own way. But many seekers, dissatisfied with or unfulfilled by traditional religion, may not realize they're not alone in their search for meaning. And many church leaders, eager to appeal to seekers, don't understand how to reach us in a structured way or how to allow us the opportunity to explore our spirituality beyond the confines of traditional religion.

So if seekers aren't lost, then what *are* we?

Seekers are people of all backgrounds who are searching for ways to live more compatibly in the world by practicing a personal spirituality that connects us with others and with a God of our own understanding. Spiritual seekers are like Janis, a woman in her late sixties who has lived in the same community for thirty years, has been married for forty-eight years, and has three children and six grandchildren. Spiritual seekers are like Paul, a widower with two college-age sons who is a clinical psychologist and an ordained minister. And seekers are like Chuck, an advertising executive, avid bird-watcher, and father of three who has been married for sixteen years. We are people who are interested, for a variety of reasons, in pursuing a spiritual path but who have found that the traditional church doesn't meet our needs.

Some of us have experienced a profound emotional upheaval that catapulted us into our search for meaning; others have been lifelong seekers, moving from one tradition to another in search of a deeper connection to the Divine. Many of us formed our first spiritual opinions as children when we recognized the inconsistencies of religion. How, for example, if we were raised in a family of mixed denominations, could we subscribe to a particular religion if it meant that only one of our parents would go to heaven and the other would be doomed to hell? Or maybe we had childhood friends of a different religion who learned in their Sunday school that they'd get into heaven while we wouldn't. This sort of irrational "pick and choose" of religious salvation is what discouraged many of us from associating with the traditional church at a young age.

Seeking may lead some people to join a traditional church where they stay and feel comfortable, leaving years later in search of more spiritual knowledge and experience. For others, seeking could lead away from traditional religion and any conventional understanding of God. The point is, all of us are seeking: for better ways to live our lives, for friends and like-minded folks, for gratifying experiences, for comfort, for direction and meaning, for hope, for an authentic life purpose, for answers, for peace of mind. Some of us embrace the teachings of the traditional church, some of us never venture anywhere near a church, and some wander from community to community, growing and integrating what we learn from each experience. As seekers, we intuitively understand that there are many ways to experience the Divine. All the world is an opportunity for exploring.

Three Types of Seekers

Though we share similar characteristics, as seekers we tend to fall into one of three different types: maybe we've had little interest in or exposure to the church; maybe we've left because we've been hurt by it; or maybe we still belong but keep searching for our own path to God outside the institution of traditional religion. Ultimately, it doesn't matter whether religion has informed our knowledge of God. What matters is that we're asking our own questions and looking for our own conception of a higher power so we can worship in a deeper and more personal way.

The first type of seeker, with limited exposure to traditional religion, is someone Christian clergy would refer to as "unchurched." These seekers have very little experience with the language and ritual of the church and may not be as heavily encumbered as other seekers with negative experiences or resentment of religion. Religious dogma has never made much sense to them, so they search for answers through contemporary readings and programs that are easy to relate to. They're spiritual wanderers searching for an experience of God in any venue that's accessible. Michele, a stay-at-home mom of two young children, describes herself as a seeker. Her story is a typical example of someone who is curious to know more about God and has a yearning for deeper spiritual experiences but who has never fully related to religion as an answer.

• MICHELE'S STORY •

For as far back as I can remember, I have been curious about God and religion. I have vivid memories of walking to school alone, having conversations with God. I attended Catholic mass with my grandmother on occasion, and although I didn't understand what I was hearing, I felt I was doing something important. I also never turned down an invitation to join a friend at church. I joined friends at their Baptist and Methodist churches. At the age of nine, I even began regularly attending a Baptist church on my own. Each Sunday a bus would come to my house and pick me up. While I waited, I recall trying to remember verses and Bible stories.

I also remember, at a very young age, asking my mother specific questions about God. I could sense, from her veiled responses, her discomfort, which I understood as a lack of belief. My father told horrific stories about attending a parochial school, so I knew he was no fan of religion, yet he never specifically addressed his beliefs either. Now that I am an adult, I know that both my parents have faith in a higher power, but neither has ever returned to the Catholic Church.

Despite being brought up in a household where spiritual beliefs were rarely, if ever, discussed, my curiosity grew. Throughout my young adulthood, I struggled with trying to find a spiritual home. I felt like an outsider. I was different from my friends who were raised in a family with strong religious beliefs, and I was uncomfortable talking about what my beliefs were because I was uncertain myself.

When a boyfriend's mother hoped to prepare me for marrying her son, I even agreed to take Catholicism classes. Of course, my desire was more out of wanting to adopt a religion than to prepare myself for a wedding. Unfortunately, the more I tried to force myself to be a part of a religious community, the more uncomfortable I felt. I didn't know the rules. I didn't know or understand the passages everyone had memorized. I hoped my love of music would somehow help me connect through the hymns, but that couldn't be forced either.

Discouraged, my search for a religious home became less of a priority, and I stopped searching for a place where I could be nourished. My desire to connect with a spiritual community seemed only to reappear during the darker moments in my life. During these times when I needed comfort and reassurance, hope that there was good in the world, I would call a friend and ask to join her at church. I wanted to hear or experience something to renew my faith in humanity and in myself. That never happened. Instead, I relived those feelings of not belonging; I felt like an imposter.

Michele's story points out the sense of longing that many seekers feel: a desire to connect meaningfully with a group and with God. Like many people, Michele was available and willing to deepen her relationship with God, but the language and liturgy of the church failed to nourish her.

With its traditional Christian vocabulary, the church can't translate its message into a workable spirituality for many contemporary seekers.

The second type of spiritual seekers have rejected religion because it has somehow failed them. They may have been regular church members who found solace in the ritual but at some point became disappointed. Perhaps their political or social beliefs differed from a particular religion or congregation, and they began to feel misunderstood. Perhaps they've tried several churches or denominations and found them boring, predictable, or just not a good fit. Perhaps the church seems hostile or judgmental, exclusive, even hypocritical in its stance. In one seeker's words, "I am turned off by ethical proclamations from the pulpit!" In any case, the traditional church doesn't meet the needs of these seekers, and their spiritual quests lead them in other directions.

Valerie, a veterinarian and the mother of two grown sons, is an example of this type of seeker. Though she spent many years involved with traditional religion, at some point she became dissatisfied and needed to move on.

• VALERIE'S STORY •

I was about twelve years old when I began to wonder if I wasn't "missing out on something important." When I asked my parents why we didn't go to church, I was given two variations of the same story—that they were made to go to church as children and found it either very unpleasant or otherwise meaningless. My parents decided not to do the same thing to my brother and me. We were free to do as we saw fit. However, my mother did accompany me once to church and was so embarrassed at dropping her monetary gift into the communion plate being passed around that we never went back.

Periodically, I'd invite myself to accompany one of my friends to church, even though my friends hardly seemed impressed with what they got from church, and they certainly never felt compelled to try to live out the Christian ethic being preached at them. They did, however, convey a strong sense of membership to a much larger group, which was in part defined by who they were—Catholic, Jewish, and so on. It was that sense of belonging that I wanted but had not the slightest idea how to achieve.

When my father was reassigned to a new post, someone recommended the fellowship group of a local Episcopal church as a way for my brother and me to make new friends. We joined (I say this in the loosest possible terms) a church where my brother and I did indeed find nice friends, a real sense of belonging, and the seeds for our individual spirituality. The priest, Father Lauder, a true visionary, led dynamic discussions about finding spirituality in the midst of problems that we struggled with—drugs, premarital sex, and the Vietnam War. He was a caring, compassionate adult who not only gave us permission to be ourselves, but raised our collective conscientiousness of who we could be.

In college I looked for other spiritual doorways and accompanied several dorm mates to a revivalist church where I watched with fascination as people waded into a pool at the front of the altar to be dunked and "saved." My friends had already taken the plunge and were urging me on, but I knew it was going to take more than just getting wet for me to feel "saved." Why did I *need* to be saved, and what was I being saved from or for?

I ended up going down several paths I wished I hadn't. My longing for membership led me into a sorority and then into association with one of the most drug-filled groups on campus. Occasionally, friends of my parents would invite me to their horse ranch surrounded by national forest in Woodland Park, Colorado. At this Rocky Mountain paradise, I watched the miracle of mares foaling and camped out under the stars. Looking up at the blue sky with white clouds covering the top of Pike's Peak, I felt its majesty and a sense of peace, calm, and contentment. I felt a great truth and strength in nature.

After college, I went to vet school, survived a failed marriage, became a loving single parent of a beautiful one-and-a-half-year-old son, and became a capable, compassionate veterinarian. Starting my own practice, marrying and divorcing again, and having a second son kept me so busy that for many years, the lack of spirituality in my life was only a fleeting thought before falling asleep at the end of very long days.

One day, a client of mine invited me to church. She picked me up, introduced me to different people, and then, to my surprise, talked through almost the entire service. Even so, something about the service resonated with me, because I remember thinking, if I had been able to really pay attention, I might have found what I needed. I attended that church long enough to become baptized, but I realized paradoxically that while I had become part of the "body of Christ," I felt almost no sense of community. The rector greeted me every week as if he had never met me before, and my fellow parishioners remained distant enough that I always felt like the newcomer.

Just as I was beginning to feel defeated again, the same friend mentioned another church, St. Andrew's, near where I lived. When I went there, the small, intimate sanctuary felt warm and welcoming. And the minister was so approachable that I felt the same kinship with him I had so many years before with Father Lauder. My attendance at St. Andrew's led to confirmation and then to serving on the church vestry.

But eventually, I felt a need to grow in my spiritual understanding. My medical training had taught me that there is more than one way of looking at and approaching things and that most organic systems and life situations are simply not constant. They fluctuate and change with the energy, intention, and conditions of the time. It made sense to me that our spirituality would do the same, that what we would find nourishing would depend on where we were on our spiritual path. When I realized there were other ways I needed to worship outside the walls of a traditional church, I knew my days at St. Andrew's were over.

Valerie's experience points out the disillusionment and disappointment many seekers feel when they realize that the answers they've been seeking aren't available through the church where they've spent so much time trying to cultivate relationships and deepen their understanding of God.

The third type of spiritual seekers are those who still have ties to the church. They may be active in their congregations, but they search outside the bounds of their denomination for deeper meaning and experience. These seekers might enjoy the ritual and familiarity of church but want to expand beyond religion to the larger realm of spirituality. They might dismiss certain aspects of dogma and view the Gospels as an important metaphorical story but don't believe that everything in the Bible should be taken as absolute truth. Or they might look to other traditions to support their current faith—a Catholic nun, for example, might practice Buddhist meditation. If these seekers don't feel supported or validated by their peers or clergy as their spiritual views expand, they might drift further away from their denomination.

Paul, an ordained minister, is one of these seekers.

• PAUL'S STORY •

Growing up in the Deep South, religion—Southern Protestantism, to be precise—was lodged within the core fabric of life. Your church was a very important institution in your life. It wasn't so much a question of whether you were an active member of a church as it was which church. With the majority of the churches being Protestant and many of those being Baptist, other religious groups were considered spiritually inferior and lacking, if not a group to target for missionary work.

My parents brought my sisters and me up in Southern Baptist churches. On Sunday we went to Sunday school and the morning worship service. On Sunday afternoons there were usually activities for young people—a youth group meeting or a choir practice—and then in the early evening there was Training Union, another Sunday school kind of activity, followed by the evening worship service. At least once a year, there was revival week. Most of these were highly emotional and were designed to stoke a new fire of commitment among the faithful and bring more members and saved souls into the fold. It was at one of these evangelical meetings that I felt something stir in me, and at the ripe age of twelve, to the strains of one of the favorite revival hymns, "Just as I Am," I went forward at the altar call and accepted Jesus as my Lord and Savior. I became a Christian.

Guilt was a major motivator, a powerful tool of the organized religion that I experienced growing up. The world was seen as evil, and one needed to set oneself apart from it to have any prospect of achieving the high prize of going to heaven when he died. Denial of the secular, tolerating life—that seemed to be the focus of our faith. People oriented to their church much like others orient to a country club where all the goings-on are highly important. Ministers were put on pedestals and were often caught up in petty controversy. The considerable amount of compassion for others was a meaningful part of church life for me. The backbiting, judgment, and political intrigue weren't.

I remember wanting to get behind the clichés I heard week after week: "Trust in Jesus; accept the Lord Jesus Christ and you will be saved," and so on. None of them seemed to tell me much. By that I mean none of them were specific enough for me. Just what was involved in attempting to embrace these admonitions? I wanted to know how to do this, how to accept, how to actively believe. Unless I wasn't paying attention, which is a distinct possibility, I don't recall getting much instruction in the specifics. What was missing, what I needed, was a spiritual experience that connected me with specific ways to live and attitudes to hold.

After undergraduate school I enrolled in a Southern Baptist seminary. My three years there were very meaningful years to me, and I owe a great debt to the friends, both professors and fellow students, I came to know there. During these seminary years I found some of the specifics I had been looking for. I began thinking about theology and spirituality in a different way, in experiential terms. My friends and I began to think about aspects of our nature as humans that appear to be givens, for example, birth and death, or the fact that as humans we require a connection to others. We began to ask ourselves how we needed to live and think if we were to live in harmony with the universe. We concluded that being true to our natures was the deepest clue about how to live meaningfully and make sense of this "predicament" of life. Isn't this the goal or destination of walking a spiritual path?

After seminary I enrolled in graduate school with the intention of pursuing a career as a parish minister, but I got onto another path and earned a degree in clinical psychology. I never became a parish minister; however, over the years I have performed "priestly" duties. I have been active in a Methodist church, led worship services, officiated at weddings and funerals, and offered the sacraments of communion and baptism. I still do these things, and I still embrace my Christian faith.

I am not anti-religious; however, religion presents obstacles of rigidity, highly prescribed ways, even ritualistic ways, of accessing spiritual truths. These prescriptive answers sometimes don't mesh well with aspects of the human experience many face. My experiential theology did not clash with my Christianity. Instead, it made my Christianity come to life. It infused my religion with spirituality. And for me, spirituality is essential. For me, spirituality is all about living well, following our instincts, taking a harmonious place within this mysterious universe.

Janis, another seeker who left organized religion in search of greater understanding, says that when she was younger, she joined a church congregation and was active on both the local and national levels for many years. Then she became a director of Christian education. She and her husband formed a house church, and later, she explored Hinduism and Buddhism. "Each of those forms of worship served us for a time," she says. "But later the more traditional forms did not serve us. There was a way I had to suspend my beliefs in order to be there."

Though Michele, Valerie, Paul, and Janis have had different experiences with religion, what makes each of them a spiritual seeker is their personal realization that they're in search of more than what the traditional church can provide. For them, religion has its limits. In each case, they felt drawn to the church in their search for God but recognized that the spiritual experience they craved could be only partially filled, if at all, by the ritual and doctrine of the church.

It may be interesting to note that many religiously devout people have gone through a process of grappling with some of the same issues that seekers do, but church people have made a decision to accommodate their beliefs within an existing religious system that has developed over thousands of years. In every religion there seems to be a few "flash points" of controversy that lead to dogmatic or political friction within the tradition. For some seekers, these controversial points are difficult to ignore— perhaps because they're actually searching for some sort of idealism that no religion offers. In fact, there are few people in mainline churches who believe in a strict and absolute adherence to *all* the teachings of their tradition, but they're content to work within the structure and framework that religion offers them.

It's also important to note that just because spiritual seekers are interested in exploring spirituality through many avenues doesn't necessarily mean their spiritual beliefs are esoteric or jumbled. Many seekers tend to have a spiritual understanding of the Divine that is, in some sense, rather mainstream. They may end up with a conventional understanding of God and life, but that understanding is the result of their own exploration and experience. They're not content to agree to a belief system that is handed to them. They want to find their own. Maybe they have an extra curiosity gene, or maybe they're just skeptical when faced with someone else's answers.

Perhaps one of the most defining characteristics of spiritual seekers is their desire to "live in the question" rather than receive rigid or dogmatic answers. They're often unwilling to subscribe to easy answers about the nature of God. For them, the search is about exploring an idea or coming toward an answer. They may not even anticipate finding a complete, all-encompassing answer, or they may know that the answers will shift and change with time. It's the process of looking that engages them as they search for spirituality rather than religion. By asking questions, they form their view of the world and come to understand their place in it. The answers they receive depend on the questions they're willing to ask.

"In my own spiritual search," says Jeff, a father of three, "I'm focused on asking better questions about the meaning of life, about our spiritual experiences, about who we are as human beings." Jeff believes that if we take time to live in the questions of our lives, we can go deeper into our experiences and our connection with spirit. It's a matter of finding the right question. Some questions, such as "Why me?" or "What's the use?" are disempowering and lead to negative answers. But there are more productive leading questions, such as "How can I grow from this?" and "Is this true for me?" that require deeper consideration. Spiritual awareness is complex and challenging. To pause in the question is to dwell in the mystery of life and God. Questioning becomes our antidote to self-deception and allows us to poke holes in the rigid or shortsighted arguments of those with whom we disagree. It is our skepticism of people or institutions that purport to know the truth that keeps us asking, "Why?" The whole concept of a static solution is absurd to us.

However, a questioning attitude, especially in fundamentalist churches, is not always welcomed. Too often, obedience and conformity are valued over questioning. Questioning can cause discomfort and challenge our assumptions and rules. Throughout history there have been instances in which those who questioned the orthodoxy, whether religious, political, or scientific, faced severe censure and sometimes even death. Galileo, for instance, began asking about how to make a better telescope with greater magnification. The answer to that question led him to ask other questions about the earth's place in the solar system. This process of questioning and discovery soon brought Galileo into direct contradiction with what the Catholic Church held to be true about the universe. Eventually, Galileo was condemned and placed under house arrest for life for believing that the Earth revolves around the sun. Contemporary seekers who dwell in personal questions that lead them toward their own understanding of the Divine have a difficult time fitting into the paradigm of absolute belief.

Like questioning, the act of seeking is a dynamic process, continually in flux. "Seek and ye shall find" means to seekers that the mere act of searching for God is a spiritual path. It isn't as if seekers try a particular path, find it doesn't work, and abandon it. Instead, they may try a particular path for a while, discover certain spiritual principles that enlighten or comfort them on their journey, and then move on to something else. They don't discard a particular spiritual teaching in favor of something better as much as they incorporate the teachings that guide them and filter out the things that fail to help them on the journey. They collect experiences and points of view from as many sources as possible. In a sense, seekers are comparison shoppers who go where the best spiritual nourishment and community can be found. It's not unusual for seekers to pick and choose from two or three religions or spiritual paths. For instance, they might simultaneously study Taoism, Buddhism, and the desert fathers and mothers of early Christianity, or they might read the Sufi poems of Rumi and Hafiz. Emerson and the transcendentalists might provide answers for a time before these seekers discover something more contemporary, such as *Conversations with God* by Neale Donald Walsch.[5] Or they might delve deeply into a religious tradition, possibly for years, before moving on to something else.

Paul explains it this way: "Sometimes we think of spirituality as segmented, that there is only a certain body of music that is spiritual, everything else is nonspiritual; that there are only certain films which are spiritual, everything else is nonspiritual. We even reserve a day of the week when we're supposed to be spiritual. But this spiritual/secular dichotomy is not something I've ever related to. We need something that points us not only to the spirituality of everyday life, but of all of life."

Paul, who has been part of religious communities, spiritual communities, and established orthodox communities, sometimes struggles with the lack of tolerance and the demand for conformity, preferring instead to be able to embrace the love and richness of spirituality within a variety of traditions. "For me," he says, "the most important tenets of my spiritual practice are those of tolerance, acceptance, and respect for everyone's spiritual path so I can learn from others."

Paul's view is common among seekers, who believe that no one tradition meets everyone's needs. For seekers, loyalty to a particular denomination is sacrificed in favor of the exploration of several possibilities. They tend to be open-minded toward all traditional and nontraditional forms of worship.

So when seekers reject institutional religion, what they're really rejecting are the methods used to communicate about God. To seekers, religion is about a belief in dogma and ritual, while spirituality is experiential and immediate—two very different things. Seekers are interested in the spiritual approach to belief in the Divine. Wade Clark Roof, in his book *A Generation of Seekers*, says that "to be religious conveys an institutional connotation: to attend worship services, to say Mass, to light Hanukkah candles. To be spiritual, in contrast, is more personal and empowering and has to do with the deepest motivations of life."[6] Spirituality is seen as the experiential side of religion. It is about experiencing life with God. Spiritual seekers are rejecting an intellectual faith in favor of a tangible relationship with the Divine. They want a faith that comes from the heart and has the power to transform a life. Despite their sometimes negative feelings about traditional religion, they share a real hunger for the genuine and personal experience of God. They are looking for something that will work in the ordinary events of life—and they'll take more than one path to find it.

The Need for Change

Despite the vast changes in society and the increasing number of spiritual seekers, the church is still trying to attract people according to a model of ministry developed several hundred years ago. If the church is to reach out to spiritual seekers, it must move beyond certain assumptions. The church erroneously presumes that what motivates church people will also motivate seekers; that the approach used to reach church people will also work as an approach to reach seekers; that seekers already understand what the church is talking about and can recognize and respond to religious language; and finally, that seekers have enough positive regard for the church to be able to respond affirmatively to its message. Unfortunately, many church people underestimate how the church is perceived by those outside of it.

This misunderstanding is critical and keeps the church from attracting and positively affecting seekers outside the Christian tradition. Lutheran pastor Walter Kallestad, in an article titled "Entertaining Evangelism," writes, "Sunday morning they sing hymns only traditional Christians know. They use religious language that only Christians can understand. Sermons are preached that become dull, boring and uninteresting to the lost because they don't have any 'assumed prior knowledge.' Church rites and rituals are practiced. Sure, much of our traditional heritage has meaning and value—but only to those who understand by having been indoctrinated to it all."[7] Kallestad makes a strong point about the irrelevance of church language in contemporary society. But even he is unable to avoid the pitfall he points out when he refers to the rest of us non-churchgoers as "the lost." That characterization is, in itself, an assumption couched in church language to which many seekers would take offense. There is an underlying assumption among Christians that those who do not "believe like us" must be lost. Even "megachurches" that strive for a contemporary approach are still operating under these same false assumptions.

But just because seekers haven't found a contemporary and practical spirituality in the church doesn't mean that they're devoid of belief or have abandoned God. Even as attendance and membership have been waning in mainline churches, there has been an enormous spiritual resurgence. A 2005 Newsweek/Beliefnet poll found that "'spirituality,' the impulse to seek communion with the Divine, is thriving," and that 79 percent of Americans under sixty years old describe themselves as "spiritual" rather than "religious."[8] Spiritual ideas and teachings have never been more accessible than they are now thanks to the Web and modern technology. Since the 1990s there has been a wave of public interest in books, articles, programs, and television specials devoted to both the historical Jesus and contemporary spirituality. A plethora of magazines, websites, chat rooms, workshops, and emergent churches have sprouted up, contributing to this renewed interest in spirituality and allowing people to connect to many diverse spiritual traditions. Books on spirituality and religion, for instance, make up the fastest-growing segment of the publishing industry. The search for God is big business.

At the start of the twenty-first century, we're in a transitional period between modernism and postmodernism that offers a great opportunity for the church to adjust its mission and engage people on a different level. The recent growth of emergent churches is an attempt by some churches to capture this interest in spirituality through new forms of worship and theological questioning. If the church has any hope of keeping pace with contemporary culture, it needs to adapt to the new spirituality and reach out to the rest of us in a way that is fresh and engaging.

CHAPTER 2

A NEW SPIRITUALITY— JOURNEYS COMMUNITY

Spiritual seekers intuitively understand that they need something else to nourish their hunger for connection and meaning on their spiritual journeys. Yet they've found that the church, at best, is an incomplete answer, a temporary resting place. Because their seeking seems to be in direct opposition to the teachings of the church, seekers often feel isolated, misunderstood, or even lost in their search.

One seeker, Pete, describes a conversation he had at a holiday dinner with an elderly aunt. "My aunt has been a devout member of a church for as long as I can remember, and for a while, I went with her every week. Over dinner I mentioned that I was looking for a community to join that was broader minded in their spiritual ideas. My Aunt Ray shook her head as if to say she knew exactly what I meant, but then she said, 'Yes, there is a lot of spirituality in religion.' She was trying to get me to go back to church with her. I knew in that instant that she didn't understand what I was talking about at all. She didn't understand the difference between spirituality and religion, and I couldn't adequately explain it. I gave up because I realized that we saw things differently and that no matter how I tried, she wouldn't be able to comprehend my need to look in another spiritual direction."

Fortunately for Pete and other seekers, this is a time of transformation. As we shift from modernism to postmodernism, certain basic beliefs about how we see the world and our relationship to it are shifting as well. Much of the conflict we've been witnessing as a society has to do with the friction between the older worldview and the new. This polarization seems to be happening on a global scale in the form of terrorism and oppression as fundamentalist ideologies lash out against the modern world. The change is not simply an abstraction. Each of us has experienced the conflict on a personal level: as a desire to fit in and agree with others in order to feel safe and accepted versus a need to assert our own opinion and sense of individuality in our beliefs. In spiritual terms, the impulse toward rigid dogma is as strong as the desire for a God who is intimate and personal. Like the opposing sides of magnets, these two ideologies seem to push and repel each other without connecting. That's where seekers find themselves spiritually—caught between rigid belief systems and a new and evolved way of experiencing spirituality.

As society changes and we shift into postmodernism, we cannot simply dismiss the older worldview as invalid. Modernism has made important contributions to our understanding of ourselves and the world. Though he didn't know it at the time, Issac Newton, when knocked on the head by an apple, helped change our way of seeing. He and others began to characterize life in scientific terms that were both rational and predictable in nature. Since then, we've come to know the world by its physical properties and seek to answer our questions through scientific study.

We shape ourselves in the image of God. In terms of our spiritual understanding, the modern period, dating from the fourteenth century, asserted the idea that God is a separate being, intervening in the world from the outside. Our human tendency is to shape ourselves in the image of our God, and since the modern period's understanding of God is that of a dominating and intervening being, this understanding translates into people exerting as much control as possible over property, money, and material objects. In a perverse sense, the visible physical world, rather than the invisible spiritual world, has become our fundamental reality. As long as we believe God is an all-powerful being, and we imitate that kind of being, our desire to dominate nature and other humans becomes our driving force. Unfortunately, this worldview has an ugly side that translates into reckless environmental practices resulting in such things as suburban sprawl and gas-guzzling SUVs. We've also witnessed capitalistic imperialism and fraud in the Enron and WorldCom scandals, and in general we have become wasteful in our ways of living.

Science studies religion. Modernism's view of God also confines our spiritual understanding. For example, if our knowledge of the world is based on material proof verified by scientific study, then the reality of God and spirituality—something that cannot be substantially measured—is called into question. That's why so much time and money have been spent studying the scientific plausibility and accuracy of ancient texts and biblical stories. In the modern worldview, the traditional church needs substantial proof to remain valid. Fundamentalism relies on absolute truth: all of our religious understanding must be true if we're to believe that any of it is true. But postmodernism looks instead for metaphorical truth—a story or experience can be true without being factually true. Postmodern spirituality emphasizes a metaphorical theology and a relational experience of God.

A shift is taking place. Modernism has made a vast contribution to our understanding of the world, but for those living in the twenty-first century, a material approach to life, as individuals and as a society, seems self-destructive. Both seekers and traditional church people—even some clergy—are adopting an increasingly complex and uncertain postmodern worldview. This shift in how we view the world and God is taking place at the grassroots level and is shaking the foundations of the church. Even as many churches resist change, others have begun to embrace postmodern beliefs and methods that seekers have long espoused.

We live in a period when ideas are quickly being transformed into actions; new communites and emergent churches are springing up to fill the gap. The church needs to learn better ways to relate to seekers and to the contemporary culture—and even to church members sitting in the pews. Some congregations and Christian emergent churches have already successfully adapted to the call for change by letting go of their traditional structures and incorporating elements of the new spirituality.

What Is the New Spirituality?

The new spirituality is a new understanding of the Divine. God is being redefined. Think of postmodern spirituality as the experiential side of religion, cutting across all traditions. Its theology, if there is one, borrows heavily from ancient and contemporary sources and is characterized as being open and creative, interested in preserving close ties to the environment, and devoted to advancing peace. The new spirituality is interested in the experience of God in daily life rather than knowledge of God as interpreted by the Bible and other sacred texts. The new spirituality replaces our belief in God as a supernatural, intervening, and transcendent force beyond our reach with a God present in us and among us as an encompassing spirit, a God within. It replaces the fear of an authoritarian king and father who has predetermined our lives with a close and loving friend who is patient, faithful, and always there for us. It replaces the judging, punishing God of the Old Testament with a God who persuades us toward better ways of being.

As our vision of the Divine changes, so does our vision of ourselves and our paths. Instead of seeing ourselves as inherently bad—sinners in need of God's forgiveness and mercy—we recognize that we're wounded and imperfect and in need of love and healing. As we pursue a patient path of inner transformation through whichever means we choose, we're offended by dos and don'ts from the pulpit. We've replaced the idea that there's only one path to salvation with the belief that there can be many paths leading to a deeper relationship with the Divine, and we embrace a sense of equality, diversity, and respect for the wisdom of all traditions. In the new spirituality, we respect each seeker's unique path and recognize that anything that moves us closer to God is worthwhile.

Creativity in the new spirituality. For us, art and music are important representations of Divine inspiration. "We get so bogged down trying to define our lives according to rational constructs," Paul says. It is the creative side of spirituality that interests him. "And life just can't be captured in rational, linguistic constructs. But art and music expand my medium of understanding. Music takes me into a wider appreciation of life."

Janis agrees. "Creativity is a way for me to be in touch with the Divine." Living creatively, day to day, moment to moment, is at its heart the most basic and authentic form of art we can practice. The new spirituality closely links inspiration to godliness, whether that inspiration comes in the form of artistic creations or through the familiar routines of every day.

God within the ordinary. Besides being creative, the new spirituality is immensely practical. As seekers expressing a desire to live spiritually here on earth, we recognize God in the small, tangible events of our daily lives. Even Jesus, who invoked images of sowing a mustard seed, attending a wedding, and baking bread, understood the ability of the Divine to reveal itself in common, ordinary events. The term "panentheism" has become a popular way to describe this idea: God is present within all things. It's not just that God *is* all things but that God is within all things as the soul of the world; we cannot understand God or the world apart from one another. The world is God; we breathe in God, or as some mystics have said, we swim in God. The opportunity to worship isn't limited to a certain day of the week but is ever present and available. In the postmodern view, God can be found everywhere in everything, not just in cathedrals or through sacred texts, but in popular culture, in our relationships with others, through our communion with nature, in the food we eat, and in the causes we support.

Our connection to the earth. The recognition of God as an encompassing spirit is actually a return to some ancient ideas. Our relationship to everything—the earth, plants, animals, and people—is giving rise to a new sense of responsibility. Environmentalism is a large part of the new spirituality as many people honor our connection to the earth and understand the importance of maintaining it. We recognize ourselves as part of a sacred, interconnected whole. For some, a walk in the woods brings closer communion with God than any church service could. Ancient seasonal observances such as solstice celebrations are being revived as seekers look back at their roots and tap into their primal awareness of being connected to the earth.

In a videotaped interview, Thomas Berry, a Jesuit priest and environmentalist, describes our connection to the earth this way: "St. Thomas says, 'Why are there so many things?' He says because the Divine could not image itself forth in any one being; it created a great diversity of things so that the perfection lacking to one would be supplied by the others and the whole universe together would participate in and manifest the Divine more than any single being whatsoever. Things cannot be [whole] simply in their isolated selves because nothing is itself without everything else."[1] Berry's point about our interconnectedness with all of life is not just one individual's interpretation of Scripture. This worldview is emerging—or resurfacing—in many places. In his book *Care of the Soul*, Thomas Moore explains that "ancient psychologists taught that our own souls are inseparable from the world's soul, and that both are found in all the many things that make up nature and culture."[2] The ecological stance of the new spirituality combines the belief that we're all interconnected with the sense that all things have their own intrinsic value.

Science and religion. The discovery that all things are connected at a deep microcosmic level has been an important development in the scientific world and has substantially impacted the way scientists now look at the biological world. They see every event, in some sense, as a microcosm that envelops the whole macrocosm of reality. Everything, that is, has an effect on everything else. Nothing is fixed. And determinism—the long-held belief that our lives are predestined—no longer makes sense. In some ways, our scientific explorations have led us back to premodern beliefs, including a recovery of the sense that life holds much deeper meanings for us than was previously held by the deterministic world view. The new spirituality reaches down to the molecular level and reinforces some ancient ideas about how we relate to the earth and to one another.

Other faith traditions. The new spirituality also takes a fresh look at religions that predate Christianity and incorporates them into contemporary life. When psychologists studied early spirituality and meditation in Buddhist and Hindu traditions, they were surprised by the wisdom of these early religions. They discovered that some of the beliefs and practices of ancient people were not superstitious after all; at the root, these ideas contained pragmatic answers to difficulties intrinsic in human relationships. For thousands of years, Buddhism and Hinduism have recognized the struggles of being human and developed early practices to overcome greed, sloth, egotism, and so on. Human frailties haven't changed much over the last two thousand years. These ancient spiritual teachings have transcended time and are just as relevant today as when they were first conceived.

A new path, not a new religion. Even as people return to ancient texts and practices, new paths are being created to answer the struggles we face as humans and to recognize our need for a new understanding of God. But the new spirituality isn't a new religion. It doesn't reject the sacred teachings of traditional religion but strives to update and assimilate them into a contemporary world. One cultural contributor to the open and tolerant postmodern view of God is Alcoholics Anonymous, which has no spiritual dogma about the Divine but has helped millions worldwide to find a personal God. When God is referred to in AA's Twelve Steps, it is always as God as we understand Him, an open-ended approach that offers a freedom of belief based on mutual respect for another's conception of God.

Experience as our guide. AA is also centered in the strength and wisdom that come from sharing personal stories. This affirmation of experience represents a significant shift in worldview. Experience is a profound teacher, and in the new spirituality, we are beginning to trust what we learn through our own life stories rather than rely on what we're told. We no longer have faith in the teachings of traditional texts or have confidence in authority figures disconnected from our personal experience. Those attracted to the new spirituality are turned off by the slightest perception of inflexibility and are alienated by glib moralizing. The new spirituality recognizes that each person is a messenger whose experience and

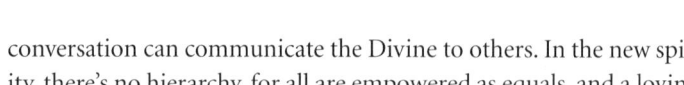

conversation can communicate the Divine to others. In the new spirituality, there's no hierarchy, for all are empowered as equals, and a loving God can express divinity though every individual.

Criticism of seeking. Even as postmodern spirituality grows and thrives, it has received a lot of criticism from church leaders and others for whom traditional religion still works. Because the new forms of worship are challenging the assumptions the church has held about its structure and mission, there are people who disagree with and fight against the changes of time. It's not just the new spirituality that has been criticized, but seekers themselves have had to defend their spiritual choices.

One thing seekers are typically criticized for is picking and choosing different spiritual paths or discarding one in favor of another. Church leaders use the derogatory term "cafeteria-style spirituality" to quickly dismiss what they see as a random and undisciplined approach to spiritual maturity. One traditionalist says this about seekers (whom he refers to as post-moderns or PoMos, a condescending term in itself): "Postmoderns are not, as a rule, happy people. They are disillusioned, disenchanted, and skeptical. The 'spirituality' of popular and post-modern culture tends to have been informed more by 'Here Comes Santa Claus' than by 'Joy to the World.' Do not expect PoMos to take kindly to the Bible's harsh treatment of sin and supposition of man's fallen-ness."[3] His view, unfortunately, is typical of people who fail to understand spiritual seekers. Their thinking is that seekers will take only the spiritual teachings that are agreeable to them and neglect other, less comfortable or less convenient teachings that lead to greater spiritual growth. In some cases, this may be true. But who is to say that longtime church members don't overlook or neglect certain doctrinal teachings for the same reason? It could be argued that in many ways, spiritual seekers are more self-motivated in their search for God than some church members who agree to a prescribed belief system. In traveling their own paths outside the traditional church, seekers have rejected the safety net, rejected the system that says, "As long as you believe and do these correct things, you will get to heaven." Instead, they have taken responsibility and accountability for their own spiritual growth with the attitude that all of life is spiritual, whether it's a song on the radio, a spiritual reading, or the laugh of a three-year-old. Seekers insist that their search is for the Divine rather than for dogma.

By criticizing the spiritual paths of seekers as undisciplined, some church leaders are also implying that seekers cannot know God in a way that is meaningful and real. They are invalidating the personal experiences of millions of people. One seeker named Barbara, who recently graduated with a certificate of advanced study in pastoral counseling, describes her path and the profound spiritual experiences she has had on her journeys.

• BARBARA'S STORY •

As a child, I remember sitting on the steps telling God about my day at school. I felt very comfortable with God, who was my friend and a good listener. I felt that he accepted me and loved me. My family and I were members of a reform Jewish temple. I attended the Sunday school and was confirmed when I was sixteen. I really enjoyed my confirmation and remember it fondly. During that year I and my classmates were required to attend Saturday Sabbath services every week. I tried to find a deeper spiritual depth and was not able to at that time. As I grew older, the whole concept of prayer became more difficult for me. My parents rarely prayed at all. Yet I was taught by my parents and the culture to live by the expectations of "shoulds and oughts." My life should follow a prescribed pattern of accommodating myself to please others.

But an awareness gnawed at me. I couldn't shake it. I was not able to find the deep level of personal devotion at temple at that time. Yet I will always be Jewish. I experimented with a Unitarian church for a while but was not satisfied. I left there and attended an Episcopal church for about a year, but I had trouble hearing the message.

I wondered, *Who am I? Where do I begin and end? Do I have the right to make my own decisions to be myself?* I was not real. It seemed I was only the reflection of others. The real me was struggling to define and validate myself in an unaccepting environment. I became so distraught because I knew I was taking a risk to defy the culture and be my real self. I became determined not to give up on myself and my life.

In time I discovered meditation. Meditation continues to be a source of peace for me. During meditation I move beyond this material world into deep within my soul to the seat of God within.

One day, while volunteering at a hospital, I was visiting patients. By late afternoon I felt depleted—just worn out. I went to the chapel and decided that I should meditate for a while. I sat in a comfortable chair and slid into a sweet meditation for about twenty minutes. As I was coming out of my meditation, I became aware of a presence behind me. The feel of it was so strong that even though I couldn't see it, I knew it was suspended over the sofa behind me. I turned to face it and said, "I love you. I love you, Lord." The deep and full love of God descended on me like a shower. The intensity of love was beyond anything I had ever experienced before. I became euphoric and felt so much love I wanted to hug and kiss the spirit. For the second time I said, "I love you, Lord. I love you," and again felt the shower of love. I was filled with great joy. It was late afternoon, and the Jewish Sabbath was starting. I felt how holy and precious this time was. I spoke to the spirit again, "Lord, I love you," and for the third time I felt the wonderful shower of love descend upon me. I became full to bursting with God's love. I felt buoyant, filled with a deep gratitude.

As I walked out of the hospital, I saw the sun setting. The sky was full of color. I felt a deep sense of joy that I had never experienced before.

Barbara's story illustrates the pressure some seekers feel to conform to prescribed religious beliefs even when those beliefs fail to meet their needs. Her searching and her need to fit in were sincere even when she felt as though she was being untrue to her authentic self. But it was through her own seeking and practice of meditation that she was able to feel a deeper connection to a personal God.

A sense of community. Another criticism of seekers and postmodern spirituality is that seekers are too self-centered in their personal search, too wedded to their individual paths and unwilling to join in a community with others. This opinion may not be as true as it was once assumed to be. Many house churches and Christian emergent churches are springing up around the country to support individuals on their paths. Though seekers tend to be skeptical about spiritual communities because of negative experiences in the past, the idea of inclusiveness is extremely important. Sometimes a group of friends will gather together or other support groups and organizations will form to encourage seekers. In fact, it's likely that our paths will eventually lead us to search for fellowship and belonging with other seekers who share a similar worldview. Journeying toward God is both individual and communal in nature. A sense of fellowship is just as important as a healthy independence. As communal beings, we inevitably find or create communities to support us. The new spirituality and the postmodern ideal allow for individualism coupled with the support of a community. Perhaps that's why the new spirituality is a booming business. Magazines, retreats, workshops, organizations, websites, and more are designed to support seekers on their journeys.

If churches wish to meet the needs of seekers in this post-denomina-tional era, they would do well to refer seekers to other traditions that might be more helpful to them on their paths. It may be humbling for churches to acknowledge that their tradition cannot meet the needs of all people, but if they truly want to help seekers on their journeys, than it is necessary for church members to acknowledge other traditions and communities that lead people into a worthwhile connection with each other and with the Divine. Any spiritual community can be a blessing if it enables people to deepen their relationship with the God of their understanding.

A New Approach

Journeys Community is one of those groups. We strive to maintain seek-ers' individuality, nurture their spiritual growth, and support them in a community of other seekers. Over the last five years, we've grown into a fellowship of people who share a common desire to experience spiritual-ity both individually and in our connections with others. Meeting weekly, Journeys gives seekers a regular opportunity to deepen a spiritual rela-tionship with one another and with a personal God of their own under-standing. Our aim is to allow people to come together in a spiritual setting and explore the spiritual dimension and purpose of their lives without being told how they should think or what they should believe.

Paul, who became an early member of Journeys Community, says, "I was drawn to Journeys Community because of its emphasis on spiritual-ity and respect for the variety of traditions that have served others in their pursuit of walking the spiritual path. It isn't a religious organization and doesn't attempt to be one. Nor is it in conflict with religion. Instead, it tries to nurture people in their spiritual journeys in a way that shows high tolerance and respect for their individual religious traditions."

What seekers find at Journeys Community is an openness to search-ing for God in a variety of ways. "I discovered, to my delight," says Valerie, a member of Journeys Community, "intellectual, spiritual, and sensory stimulation beyond anything I could have imagined. It was OK to ques-tion, explore, and compare spiritual teachings from many sources and religions, with others who like me did not find traditional liturgy and worship very inspiring or enlightening."

Journeys strives to provide spiritually stimulating ideas and content for seekers to examine their beliefs in a way that is personal, immediate, sometimes unconventional, often practical, and deeply meaningful. As a means of engaging seekers and helping them on their paths, Journeys Community is a model of the new spirituality.

The Love of Jesus and the Wisdom of Paul

As a model for a postmodern spiritual community, Journeys Community appeals to seekers in a way that emulates the approach of Jesus and St. Paul. In its efforts to include seekers regardless of religious background or beliefs, Journeys Community is following Jesus' example of nonsectarian acceptance.

With his all-encompassing love, Jesus was most interested in those who had been ostracized or tyrannized by the traditions of religious men. His message reached out to everyone: outcasts, Samaritans, tax collectors, Gentiles, women, the poor, the sick, and lepers. Jesus ministered not to the religious but to the outsiders.

As Huston Smith writes:

> Having concluded that Yahweh's central attribute was compassion, Jesus saw social barriers as an affront to that compassion. So he parlayed with tax collectors, dined with outcasts and sinners, socialized with prostitutes, and healed on the Sabbath when compassion prompted doing so. This made him a social prophet, challenging the boundaries of the existing order and advocating an alternative vision of the human community.[4]

Jesus' choice of friends landed him in hot water. He was accused of befriending sinners, drunkards, and worse. Still, he continued to preach a message of love on the highways, in the marketplaces, on the hills, and in the wilderness—wherever people had been rejected by the mainstream. But his methods conflicted with the religious leadership of the day, which he saw as legalistic, abusive, and oppressive. In the end, it was this conflict that finally killed him.

But the disciple Paul, one of Christianity's earliest apostolic witnesses, continued to carry Jesus' message of love in his travels, engaging seekers on a cultural level in a way that serves as a model for Journeys Community. Paul journeyed more than ten thousand miles and preached from Syria to Cyprus, connecting people with the gospel—the good news—within the context of their lives. He recognized immediately that if he were to touch people with the news of Jesus, he'd need to reach out to them through the culture in which they lived.

In his letter to the Christians at Corinth, Paul illustrates his radical approach in preaching the gospel to a non-Jewish culture.

For though I am free with respect to all, I have made myself a slave to all, so that I might win more of them. To the Jews I became as a Jew, in order to win Jews. To those under the law I became as one under the law (though I myself am not under the law) so that I might win those under the law. To those outside the law I became as one outside the law (though I am not free from God's law but am under Christ's law) so that I might win those outside the law. To the weak I became weak, so that I might win the weak. I have become all things to all people, that I might by all means save some. (1 Cor 9:19–22)

Paul insisted that the good news of Christ had to be adapted to the worldview and culture of the people who were hearing it. In Acts 15, Paul opposes those in the Jerusalem church who insist that these new converts to Christianity become like Jews in order to be acceptable to God. If the Gentiles were going to be included as Christians, Paul knew they had to be accepted without having to give up their own culture. Paul argued that even pagans, thought to be far from the Divine, could know God. He understood the same thing the Christian church is struggling to recognize today: that the message of the church needs to be brought to the people through the culture and the language that they understand.

That's not to say that Journeys Community is attempting new and creative ways to bring Christianity to seekers. If that were the case, Journeys would be little more than an innovative outreach ministry of the church. In fact, what Journeys Community is emulating in Paul's approach is the willingness to accept people where they are in their lives, recognizing that God is present and available in the wider culture, not just in the doctrines of the church.

Paul's understanding of seekers made him a visionary thinker. He synthesized Stoicism of the Greco-Roman world, Judaism, and Christian theology as he strove to relate to the people he met. He was like a chameleon, joining several groups and embracing many ideas in his efforts to spread the vision of God's love. We still see the results of his efforts. Because Paul allowed people to worship in a way that was consistent with their cultural heritage, pre-Christian cultural traditions were adapted by—and often combined with—Christian theology. The birth of Jesus, for instance, is celebrated during the time of year when many ancient people observed the solstice and celebrated the Roman holiday Saturnalia—a holiday marked by festivity, gluttony, and gift-giving. Even a lighted Christmas tree is the modern equivalent of an ancient practice. Christmas as we know it is a reworking of earlier customs that have been reinterpreted and layered with Christian symbolism and meaning. Easter is another example of a Christian observance with pre-Christian roots. The church tied Jesus' resurrection and the promise of rebirth and new life to pagan observances that honored the coming of spring. The early church adopted these ancient celebrations, giving them new symbolic significance as a way of attracting more people to the gospel. In this way, the early church understood the power of culture; it recognized that the culture is inseparable from the worldview on which people base their lives.

Throughout history, Christians have tried to adapt to the local culture. During the Reformation period, Martin Luther recognized that God would accept people who spoke German and worshiped in ways that were consistent with German customs—their worship didn't have to be in Latin to be acceptable to God. Luther translated the Roman mass into German to help people connect more immediately with God. Likewise, the discovery that God could be worshiped just as well through the English culture and language partially led to the Anglican break with Rome. In our own time, there are many examples of pagan peoples who have converted to Christianity through the efforts of missionaries yet still retain many of their former cultural and spiritual beliefs. Haitians, for example, are primarily Catholic, but their Catholicism is at times indistinguishable from their native spiritual practice of voodoo. Their Catholic saints have been imbued with the characteristics of other deities, while their practice of Haitian voodoo is laden with Catholic symbolism and imagery. Throughout the ages, seekers and church people alike have discovered again and again that the Divine accepts them within their own culture. Furthermore, using the culture to relate to God only serves to enhance and deepen one's belief and worship rather than diminish it. This spirit of adaptability is one of the defining characteristics of the Journeys Community.

Because they know the concept of God is adaptable and available to all, seekers understand that they can practice a spirituality that is not prescribed by others but based on their own experiences. So it's no longer necessary to attract people to the traditional church to engage them spiritually. Rather, spirituality can be brought to them in an experiential way through contemporary culture: movies, popular music, books, theater, and so on. Contemporary culture that is shuffled into new arrangements forms what Tom Beaudoin calls *bricolage* in his book, *Virtual Faith: The Irreverent Spiritual Quest of Generation X.*[5] *Bricolage* is a French word meaning the loose combination of tools and improvisations to solve a problem. Spiritual bricolage, then, is a piecing together of images, symbols, doctrines, texts, religious beliefs, moral codes, and pop culture as a way to encounter the Divine. Yet even as some churches offer contemporary worship services as part of their outreach ministry to seekers, they fail to move beyond the traditional church teachings.

As a tangible example of spiritual bricolage, Journeys Community combines live and recorded popular music, movie clips, photographs, art, literary excerpts, spiritual readings and poems from all traditions. The services also include a silent meditation and a symbolic meal designed around a different theme each week. Journeys consciously refrains from espousing a particular "religious" view but allows seekers to experience the bricolage on their own terms, as the services borrow from all genres, from the music of U2, the Beatles, and Louis Armstrong, to clips from movies such as *The Shawshank Redemption, African Queen*, and *Schindler's List*, to readings from T. S. Eliot, Mother Teresa, and the Buddhist monk Thich Nhat Hanh. Journeys Community uses contemporary culture to touch upon universal themes such as hope, gratitude, and forgiveness. While the spiritual topics may be the same as what you'd find in a traditional church, the method for exploring these themes is universal, experiential, and engaging.

Journeys Community was envisioned by Episcopal priest Harry Brunett. While working on his doctorate in Congregational Development, Harry began considering ways the Episcopal Church could appeal to people of all ages who were searching for spiritual purpose in their lives but had been unable to find meaning in the traditional church. In 1999 he recruited a ministry team, and together they designed four prototype services. The end result, Journeys Community, has been meeting regularly every Sunday since September 2001, attracting some fifty people to its services each week.

While separating itself in design and theology from the traditional church, Journeys Community brings together seekers of all backgrounds and ideologies. As a model for other seeker communities, Journeys Community recognizes itself as something other than a church.

A Church That Isn't a Church:
The Theology of Journeys Community

Though we reject rigid dogma and steer away from prescribing answers to spiritual questions, we do have some basic tenets to guide us. Our experience has shown us the importance of recognizing the practical everyday experiences of God, honoring our personal stories, and acknowledging that each of us is a messenger; we ask questions and take personal responsibility for our own spiritual paths; and we understand the human spirit is closely connected to the culture.

God Is Revealed in Ordinary Life

Journeys Community believes that God is revealed to us through our personal experiences of everyday life. A person may come to know God through some life-changing, event, but mostly our relationship with the Divine springs from the ordinary events of our lives. Common objects and daily routines can evoke deep spiritual truths. Frederick Buechner, in *Listening to Your Life*, says it this way:

> There is no event so commonplace but that God is present within it, always hidden, always leaving you room to recognize Him or not recognize Him. . . . If I were called upon to state in a few words the essence of everything I was trying to say both as a novelist and as a preacher, it would be something like this: Listen to your life. See it for the fathomless mystery that it is. In the boredom and pain of it no less than in the excitement and gladness: touch, taste, smell your way to the holy and hidden heart of it because in the last analysis all moments are key moments, and life itself is grace.[6]

Seeing God in the ordinary touches the holy in a way that gives holiness to everything we touch. One seeker named Bill sees all of life as a spiritual journey. He describes his experiences and his relationship to God in a way that is practical and easy to understand.

• BILL'S STORY •

As I dressed in white robes as an altar boy trying to remember the parts of mass, I didn't feel God. But as I sat in church in silence after everyone left, I felt God.

When I was sixteen and I watched my dad leave the house forever, I cried in my room and I felt God. As I watched my mother struggle as a single parent, I didn't feel God, but as I bonded more strongly to my sisters and brother, I felt God.

As I drowned my sorrows, frustrations, pain, and loneliness in drugs and alcohol, and when I drove down the highway on Christmas morning drunk, lonely, and in tears, I didn't feel God. But as I played drums, connected with friends, and created art through music, I felt God.

When I learned about different religions, I was confused about God. As I traveled for many years alone in the dark with the stars above, I was aware of God.

As I got my first job after college, bought things, and went places, I didn't feel God. But when I met my wife, I felt God. As I stood at the altar and watched my wife place her step toward mine in life, I felt God. As I held my new son in my arms, looked into his eyes, and connected deeply, I felt God. As I continued to search and redefine my life, I felt God. As my second son was born and a new love was present, I felt God. And as my third child, a daughter, was born and tears ran down my face, I felt God. As I cared for my family, I saw God in every minute.

As I blessed my auto journey on a rainy day, I felt God. As my body was tossed thirty feet into the air from an auto accident on that same rainy day, I felt God, angels, and hands lift me up to land perfectly unharmed.

When airplanes smashed into the World Trade Center on 9/11, I felt God's presence. When I read the letter of termination from my sales job, I didn't feel God. As I picked pumpkins and worked on a farm to pay bills, I felt God. As I walked through the snow alone, jobless and feeling nothing, as I stood in line at a food shelter, I didn't feel God. As I looked at my three children and wife sleeping each night, I felt God was near but still far away. When I pulled a knife out of drawer and thought for a moment of hurting myself, I felt the force of God push it away. As I went back to the food shelter and picked out fresh breads and yams, I felt blessed by all that God had done for me.

As I continue to struggle to pay bills and provide for the family, I feel God. As I love and kiss my family on Valentine's Day, bringing them home-made cards, I feel God. As I write this I see God has always been with me, next to me, within me, and within others. As my breath moves in and out, so does my awareness of God and her presence.

Bill's experience of a God who is interwoven with his own life sums up the practical, day-to-day theology of Journeys Community. In taking spiritual stock of our days, reflecting on both the good and the bad, we're able to witness the presence of the Divine in our lives. We seek to experience God not through knowledge, creeds, and dogmas, but through direct encounters with the Divine in our ordinary lives.

We Are All Messengers

We believe that each of us is an expression of the Divine and that all of us are one. Or as Thomas Berry says, "The whole universe together would participate in and manifest the Divine more than any single being whatsoever."[7] There is a Divine presence within us, not just above us, and our personal stories can reveal who God is in the world. That makes us messengers, teachers to one another through the way we live our lives. To paraphrase Gandhi, "We must be the change we wish to see in the world."[8] Or as recovering alcoholics in AA say to each other as a reminder to live according to the Twelve Steps, "You might be the only big book someone else sees."

We Must Be Authentic and True to Ourselves

To be able to live a true faith, Journeys Community believes we must honor our authentic selves. By digging deeper into ourselves, past our fears and insecurities, past our material concerns, we are able to get closer to God. To become authentic we must get to the root of who we are—to do that we must learn to value our own vulnerability and practice intimacy, compassion, and honesty in our relationships with others. We have to honor our true worth. This process of becoming authentic leads us into a deeper relationship with the Divine.

God Includes Everyone

Because we're all seen as expressions of God, Journeys Community is inherently inclusive. We understand that God touches each of us differently, so a sense of belonging and acceptance is paramount to the theology of our community. Because many of us have felt excluded from the traditional church, we welcome everyone, regardless of their spiritual beliefs, which encourages us to learn from—and be transformed by—the spiritual truths of all traditions. Our attitude is a reformulation of the key principal, "God as you understand God," a basic tenet of Alcoholics Anonymous. Many Journeys Community members draw their spiritual understandings from Judaism, Christianity, Hinduism, Buddhism, and Islam as well as from the ancient mystics and Native American customs. In fact, there's no inconsistency between other religious traditions and Journeys Community. Journeys works in tandem with any faith to deepen the connection to God. The Journeys ministry team recognizes the need to remain open to new ways of seeing and experiencing spirituality, which is one of Journeys Community's most pronounced departures from the teachings of the Christian church. But this openness is an essential value in the formation of a seeker community.

God Is Found in the Deepest Questions

Our openness to other traditions leads us to ask questions about God and life, and that type of questioning brings many seekers back each week. "Where is God in this?" is the most important question that is asked. The poet Rainer Maria Rilke writes:

> I beg you . . . to have patience with everything unresolved in your heart and try to love the questions themselves as if they were locked rooms or books written in a very foreign language. Don't search for the answers, which could not be given you now, because you would not be able to live them. And the point is, to live everything. Live the questions now. Perhaps then, someday far in the future, you will gradually, without ever noticing it, live your way into the answer.[9]

In creating every service, the ministry team asks questions of itself to get to the heart of whatever topic we are examining. Journeys Community also poses significant questions to its members about various aspects of the quest for a Spirit-based life. It's no coincidence that the words "question" and "quest" are, at root, the same word. A questioning attitude is at the heart of many of the world's religious traditions. This attitude comes from the recognition that spiritual awareness is complex and challenging. As seekers, we're not content to be given answers; we must ask our own questions to discover our own truths. Socrates set the standard for a questioning attitude; the Socratic method encourages us to ask probing questions in a give-and-take format that leads us to a fuller understanding. In Buddhism the goal of questioning is to take us beyond our own experience and see the world in a deeper way. In an address to the British Parliament, the Dalai Lama said, "Don't believe easily. Deeper awareness, genuine awareness demands questioning."[10] Likewise, Jewish traditions are based on thousands of years of commentary, conversation, and questioning about the meaning of the Torah. It's a conversation that echoes across the ages. In Judaism, intellectual questioning is not only tolerated; it's encouraged. The four gospel accounts of Jesus' life list almost three hundred questions that Jesus asks to instruct his listeners in order that they might teach themselves. Among many other questions, Jesus asks, "What do you want me to do for you?" "Who do you say that I am?" "Why do you call me good?" "Couldn't you stay awake?" "Why have you forsaken me?" "Who are you looking for?"

If we, as seekers, take the time to live into the questions of our lives, as Rilke suggests, we can enter into a deeper understanding of grace. To pause in the question is to dwell in the mystery of life and of God.

God Is Found by a Variety of Paths

In many ways, Journeys Community is a framework within which people explore and nurture their spirituality and progress on their own life paths. In many of our experiences with the traditional church, seekers have a sense that we must temporarily set our day-to-day lives aside and participate as an Episcopalian or Baptist or Catholic; we might know the pattern of the service and recite all the prayers by heart; and perhaps, if we're regular church members, we may love the ritual and feel comfortable in the pattern. But for those of us who are still seeking, traditional church services don't really allow us to process the information and find personal meaning. Church is more about plugging into an established meaning and practice that exists independently of us. But at Journeys Community, there's an unspoken acknowledgment that seekers need only take from the services the truths that speak to them. It's a theology of "take what is most meaningful to you and leave the rest." Journeys understands that each of us is responsible for ourselves and for traveling our own spiritual paths. Journeys Community creates a space to consciously examine our spiritual lives and to experience the Divine in relation to others. These spiritual tenets aren't esoteric, limited to the extreme thinking of certain "new age" groups. They're beliefs that are generally accepted among seekers as a normal way of seeing the world and our relationship to the Divine.

God Is Found in Popular Culture

What sets Journeys Community apart from the traditional church and from other postmodern spiritualities, more than anything, is its conscious use of popular culture to directly connect to the human spirit. Just as people express their hopes, fears, dreams, and desires through the popular culture, Journeys purposely taps into that culture to create experiential services where members can individually and collectively connect deeply with the God of their understanding. As Tom Beaudoin suggests, being attentive and responsive to contemporary culture can "teach us something about God, faith, and religious practice."[11]

Though many traditional churches have formed seeker ministries and use references to popular culture as a means of connecting with people, their ultimate goal is to convert the seeker into a regular church member.

It is important to note that Journeys Community is not a traditional church with cultural references added to the format to make it relevant. Instead, Journeys Community services are specifically designed around a different theme each week, depending on how the culture intersects with that theme. For instance, a service about forgiveness might highlight a clip from the movie *Dead Man Walking* and include songs such as Sarah McLaughlin's rendition of the prayer of St. Francis and a rendition of The Beatles' song "Let It Be." A Journeys Community service usually includes a combination of spiritual readings, film clips, music, a reflection or personal story delivered by a community member or someone on the ministry team, a meditation, a symbolic meal, and a "spiritual convergence," which is a way for community members to interact directly with the theme. But even these elements change regularly.

The Role of Ritual and Ceremony: A Spiritual Convergence

Though many in the traditional church view postmodern spirituality as abstract and esoteric, they might be surprised to learn how significant a role ritual and ceremony play in the new spirituality. Personal story, metaphor, and symbol in particular are powerful tools in connecting us with the deeper realities of our lives. Rituals, whether in a spiritual service or in our daily lives, symbolically act out our fundamental beliefs. The physical action of performing a ritual reminds us of our values and connects us to the whole of life. At Journeys Community, the spiritual convergence is a conscious effort to connect with the experience of God. Each of our weekly services contains a number of ritual elements.

Storytelling

We recognize personal stories as one way to reach seekers. In our services, we emulate Jesus, who recognized the power of stories to reveal deeper truths. Jesus spoke about common aspects of life in the parables he told and used the imagery, culture, people, situations, and language of first-century Israel. These metaphorical narratives weren't meant to be taken literally but were meant to illuminate the truth of an idea. People could relate to the stories Jesus told because he spoke about the world they knew. Parables and stories continue to work because they intuitively provoke us to wonder about our own lives and how we can apply a story's deeper meaning.

At Journeys Community, rather than preaching to seekers about what we should or shouldn't do or believe to be acceptable to God, the ministry team has made a conscious choice to focus on our own personal experience of God. By telling stories about our own struggles and triumphs; asking questions of ourselves, of God, and of others; and sharing the wisdom of our own life experience, the ministry team has been able to involve more of us in the process of recognizing God in daily life. But personal stories aren't limited to the experiences of the ministry team. Community members have also become involved in sharing stories and composing spiritual reflections centered around a particular theme. Sometimes a service is designed to allow many members to share their personal stories as part of a group discussion. This opportunity to share some of our own experiences of God in a group setting would rarely if ever happen in a traditional church service. One seeker, Colleen, expresses her gratitude for a place where she can express herself openly:

> My conscious spiritual path has begun with Journeys Community. This is the first place I have consciously chosen to celebrate my spirituality and deepen my sense of connection with other people's spiritual expression. Journeys Community is also the first place I have consistently ventured to speak publicly the truth of my feelings in the moment: I feel happy; I feel sad; I feel angry; I feel lonely. It is the first place in my experience where I have come—in the words of Walt Whitman—"to know the universe itself as a road, as many roads, roads for traveling souls."

At Journeys Community, we tell stories of healing, of daily interactions with the world and lessons gleaned from those encounters; we speak about moments of gratitude and awareness of God's presence. Many seekers share their experience with prayer and meditation, and everyone learns from each other. These personal narratives display an authenticity that is believable, accessible, and inspiring. Stories serve to keep the services experiential rather than prescriptive. In this way, the services move the relationship with God from the head into the heart.

Ritual Convergence

A further expression of the willingness to connect with God comes through a "spiritual convergence." The spiritual convergence is a symbolic vehicle for connecting the community with each other and with God. It changes from week to week depending on the theme: sometimes community members write letters to themselves, build altars, join in prayer, laugh, reenact a Benedictine ceremony of forgiveness, meditate during a Japanese tea ceremony, or recite a litany of thanks one by one around the room. These symbolic gestures connect seekers with their deeper values and with the God of their understanding. For instance, in a service about fear and faith, the ministry team stacked bricks on a stage before the service to represent the walls of fear we build around ourselves to keep others and God away. When it came time in the service for the spiritual convergence, community members came forward and tore down the wall, brick by brick, then placed the bricks on the floor in a line to create a symbolic pathway to God. In other services, the spiritual convergences are more thoughtful and personal as the experience of God moves inward. Acting out a symbolic ritual is an immediate and tangible way of bringing the love and peace of God into the lives of those who participate.

Symbolic Meal

The symbolic meal provides yet another opportunity for seekers to connect with the theme, with God, and with each other. The symbolic meal always represents the spiritual nourishment—the food of God—that sustains us through our lives. Like the spiritual convergence, the actual meal changes from week to week depending on the theme. For example, in a service about the importance of community, the symbolic meal might be a bunch of grapes characterizing our individuality in the midst of our connection with others. For a theme about persevering on a spiritual path, the symbolic meal might be trail mix for the road ahead. Very often, the ministry team has served simple bread and olive oil for spiritual sustenance, but more elaborate meals have also been planned, such as Persian cakes to celebrate the coming of spring, or traditional Jewish fare to confront the meaning of regret and repentance. Sometimes community members come forward to receive the meal as they would at a traditional communion service; other times they pass the meal, serving each other to reinforce their spiritual connection and to recognize the Spirit of God within each of us.

Variety

One of the most intriguing aspects of Journeys Community is the fact that the services differ from week to week—no two are exactly alike. Journeys avoids a prescribed and predictable format to keep its services fresh and engaging. The rhythm and flow of each service are determined

by the content. One week, a peaceful reading might lead into a reflection and personal story, while another week, the film clip becomes the emotional heart of the service. Some services are designed around music, while others center on silent meditation. Seekers respond well to the changing format because it keeps them aware of and thoughtful about the ever-changing presence of God in their lives. As one community member says, "We are never bored; it's always a surprise."

Though there is no such thing as a typical Journeys Community service, a Sunday morning might begin with community members quieting themselves in a candlelit room by listening to recorded meditative music (perhaps Mozart or Buddhist chanting or nature sounds). Usually, a series of images and quotes that introduces the day's theme is projected onto a screen in the front of the room. The quotes are a popular part of Journeys Community services, inviting members to engage with the theme and contemplate their lives.

A fundamental aspect of the Journeys Community service is the live music. Three musicians—vocalist, guitarist, and keyboard player—transform pop music into a spiritual experience. As much as possible, the ministry team tries to find contemporary music that crystallizes the spiritual meaning of the theme. A random sampling of artists whose music is performed at Journeys includes Bonnie Raitt, Sting, George Harrison, Bette Midler, Emmylou Harris, Louis Armstrong, and Ziggy Marley. The musicians also perform music with deeper roots, such as gospel music, old spirituals, bluegrass, Native American chants, classical music, and African drumming. Part of the experience of the music comes from reading the lyrics that are projected onto a screen. Anyone who wishes to can sing along. Many Journeys Community members comment that they never realized how spiritual contemporary music could actually be until they read the words.

Film clips are a popular element of Journeys Community services as well. Dramatic film clips often reinforce a spiritual message, whether of forgiveness, hope, perseverance, or compassion. For instance, *The Shawshank Redemption* illustrates the power of hope; *Cider House Rules* reflects on the loneliness of orphanhood; *Fahrenheit 451* emphasizes the power of words. Journeys Community has also used clips from *On Golden Pond*, *Gandhi*, *The Simpsons*, and *Charlie Brown*. Journeys Community will use any art form if it helps to illustrate the power of the theme. In the new spirituality, image is as much a part of our lives and collective story as text was for previous generations.

Likewise, spiritual readings are drawn from many sources. Journeys has used the prayer of St. Francis as a meditation, an excerpt from Nelson Mandela's autobiography to discuss freedom, and a passage written by Mother Teresa to contemplate compassion. Traditional texts such as the Bible and the Bhagavad Gita have also been used. Any reading is appropriate if it enhances the theme and speaks to the heart: the poetry of T. S. Eliot, Kahil Gibran, and the Sufi mystic Rumi; the meditations of Thich Nhat Hanh and Rabbi Harold Kushner; explorations by Joseph Campbell; and fiction by Herman Hesse and Dr. Seuss, among many others. The readings reflect different views of the human condition and address the questions seekers encounter as they explore their relationship with the Divine.

In its almost endless variety, Journeys Community truly embodies the concept of spiritual bricolage. Journeys uses all aspects of the culture to explore a spiritual theme in a way that is easy for seekers to relate to and understand. As much as Journeys Community is formed by contemporary culture, the services are not just a rapid firing of images and music to engage seekers. We make a profound effort to include personal stories, metaphors, and symbols that touch the core of life and send a deeper message about God in our midst.

A Model Community for Seekers

A full relationship with God can't exist in a vacuum—to find God, people need to engage with the larger community. With its growing membership, Journeys recognizes the necessity of connecting with others while honoring an individual's choices and spiritual path. One member of Journeys Community, Sally, describes her sense of connection this way:

> It really is about all of us supporting each other's journey. One snowy Sunday morning I called the "inclement weather phone number" for Journeys Community to find out if the service was still meeting. Just as I hung up, Harry called me. He wanted to let me know personally that the service had been canceled that morning. In that phone call, we connected. At Journeys Community we stay in touch. We appreciate each other. In the two years I have been coming to Journeys Community, its members have been very supportive. When I needed surgery, Harry and Elizabeth were there with me and my daughter. When I couldn't drive and needed rides, Mickey was there, sometimes on a moment's notice. We are a community of people helping each other. How much more accepting could spirituality be? It's as if we bow silently to each other, honoring each other's spirit on the journey.

The ministry team of Journeys Community knows it is appealing to people who have had negative experiences with the traditional church and who are weary of being preached at. The team also knows that seekers are not natural "joiners." However, all spiritual paths lead to the need for community, and that's where Journeys Community positions itself: as a church that is something more than a church. It is a model for other seeker communities.

Yet Journeys Community is indistinguishable from a traditional church in the way that it sees its responsibility to the larger community. Not only does Journeys have a large and thriving membership, but it pursues opportunities for greater fellowship by hosting biweekly discussion groups where members can join to explore their spirituality in a more intimate setting with the support of fellow seekers. Journeys is also committed to serving the larger community through friendship, pastoral care, outreach projects, and compassionate giving. All of these activities have deepened the spiritual relationships among the seekers who find their way to our community.

The traditional church has much to learn from Journeys Community. In the chapters that follow, we'll share ways to develop and support a seeker community for those who are eager to move beyond the traditional understanding of church.

CHAPTER 3

A MODEL FOR BUILDING SEEKER COMMUNITIES

The success of Journeys Community is a testament to the hunger for communities that nourish seekers' quests for the Divine. Many churches and organizations have already expressed interest in creating seeker communities to complement the services they already provide. But as the ministry team of Journeys Community can attest, effective seeker communities require individual planning and dedication. The story of how Journeys Community came into being provides an important framework for other organizations to follow if they wish to develop a flourishing seeker community in their area. Here's a look at our beginnings.

Early Roots

Though Journeys Community took three years of careful research and development before it was fully realized, its genesis began many years before that. In fact, if you ask Harry Brunett about Journeys Community, he'll tell you it has taken a lifetime. It was shaped by the early experiences of Harry himself, and it came to fruition in his thesis for his Doctor of Ministry degree from Seabury-Western Theological Seminary. His thesis, "A Seeker Ministry for the Next Generation," became the community's vision and blueprint.

Harry, who spent his childhood in an orphanage, credits those early years with helping to define his spiritual path. "A lasting memory of the orphanage for me was at dinnertime," he says. "The children who had been sent to the home sat at a small table off to the side while all the other children and adults were included at the large main table. I could never understand why some were included in the family and others were not. As I grew up, I never forgot those experiences and found myself drawn to people who were relegated to the margins of society." As an adult, Harry developed a passion for social justice and a need to create a welcoming, safe place where everyone felt included. In the 1960s he connected his early experiences at the orphanage with his call to ministry and became a priest in 1962. He served in two parishes for five years; then in 1966 he became a civil rights worker and community organizer in Baltimore and Chicago before returning to parish ministry. He says, "This commitment to social justice was defining for me because it enabled me to respond to those who were not included at society's table."

During the thirty years Harry spent outside the church, he became more and more aware of people who were looking for a spiritual dimension and purpose to their lives but had been unable to find a spiritual home. He realized how many people felt excluded from traditional faith: they'd never been exposed to the church, had tried church but found it unfulfilling, or were interested in expanding their spirituality beyond the teachings of traditional religion. Harry recognized a common desire among many people to explore spiritual paths individually and in relationship with others. His drive to help people find their voices led him back to the seminary in search of new and creative ways to assist and include people in their search for God. Journeys Community is the result.

Developing a Plan

Planning and development began in 1999, and by September 2001, Journeys Community was in full swing, hosting weekly services and steadily growing. With no previous model to follow, the ministry team faced a steep learning curve.

Advertising executive—and fellow seeker—Chuck Donofrio understood Harry's vision immediately and became an early member of the design team. Here is Chuck's story.

• CHUCK'S STORY •

My spiritual experience probably began when I was six years old in Sunday school, where we found a praying mantis cocoon. The teacher said over the weeks something would happen with the cocoon. I didn't know what that meant, but one Sunday morning in the school there were all of a sudden thousands of tiny praying mantises everywhere! I recall feeling that it was unbelievable and miraculous; it was extraordinary in a way that I could relate to. And because it was connected with church, somehow it was connected with God.

When I was in the sixth grade, I began to sing in the boys choir at St. Paul's School and Old St. Paul's Episcopal Church. I had no particular interest in religion, but because we sang, we had to sit in the choir stalls in a big formal church with a huge organ. We were expected to be professional—we got paid. Singing was a wonderful experience. There was something very moving about it that I loved. I learned the liturgy from hearing it every Sunday for six years, but I didn't have any great belief or disbelief in it.

I have always been predisposed to nature as a way of experiencing God. Nature for me is always so filled with wonder. That continues to this day. When I was about fifteen years old, I had a hallucinogenic experience that was incredible. I was sitting in a field, and some aspect of the grass just captivated me. I was seized with the most vivid realization that I was connected to the grass and everything else in the world; that I was in all things and that all things were in me. It wasn't a religious experience, but it was a spiritual experience that was extraordinarily moving. The feeling of peace was incredible. Of course, I discount experiences that are caused by drugs, but on the other hand, this experience became part of my understanding of the world and had a great deal of impact on me.

My path continued into drugs and alcohol, but eventually those hedonistic experiences became less and less satisfying. My alcoholism also became a physical, mental, and spiritual problem of not being true to myself and of being in decline. I hit the bottom of my drug and alcohol use, and in that bottom was an experience that happened in an instant that got me from being a drinker to a nondrinker, and it was clearly a spiritual experience. I had what seemed like a hallucination but wasn't. I saw myself going into a tunnel of black, moving into this darkness where things in my life were falling away until eventually I came face-to-face with this utter empty blackness which I assumed was death. In that moment, I felt as if a weight came off my body. Something happened to me that day that gave me a chance to change. From that day to this, I haven't had a drink or drug. I became involved with different organizations that gave me a look at a new kind of spirituality.

Chuck's new spirituality led him back to the Episcopal Church for a while, where he was asked to join the Mission Strategy Group of the Diocese of Maryland. The Diocese wanted to reach out to people who had a spiritual hunger but didn't find the church to be of use. "That, to me, is the height of altruism," Chuck says. "It was wonderful to see the church embrace this mission for people who might never become church members." It was in the Mission Strategy Group that Harry and Chuck began to plan Journeys Community.

Recruiting a Team

Before the new ministry even had a name, Harry was faced with the challenge of recruiting a ministry team who understood his vision. He didn't want to form a seeker community that served as a back door to the traditional church, a contemporary facade for religion, or a version of the traditional church in disguise. He wanted a community that allowed seekers to believe in and respond to a God of their own understanding. He wanted to create an atmosphere of acceptance for seekers to explore their spirituality on their own terms. Gradually others, one by one, were attracted to the idea of creating a seeker community.

Financial Issues

Research and development for Journeys Community were supported by the Episcopal Diocese of Maryland. But both Harry and Chuck realized that they'd have to expand beyond the walls of the church if they were to attract people for whom the church was not an answer. As Chuck pointed out to the church leaders at a committee meeting, the church could not promote itself to people who were uninterested in church—that method had already failed. If, on the other hand, the church was earnest in its wish to attract seekers, it would need to support something that seekers would be attracted to—a spiritual setting that was open and inclusive and unrelated to the traditional church. For obvious reasons, this was a difficult concept for Harry to convey to church leaders and to his former congregation, and he met with some resistance. While Harry received support and encouragement from the church hierarchy and individual Episcopalians, others disagreed with his approach and his mission. Some feel that Journeys Community shouldn't stand apart from the Episcopal Church—in a time of scarce resources, they reason, the church shouldn't put its funding into efforts that don't attract new people into the pews or more money in the collection plate. But in a move uncharacteristic for many traditional churches, the Episcopal Diocese of Maryland, expecting nothing in return except the satisfaction of reaching out to seekers, agreed to help.

Surveying the Scene

While a ministry team was being formed, Chuck conducted surveys to learn more about seekers and determine what kind of audience he and Harry were trying to attract. He gathered spiritual biographies and asked questions about people's earliest memories of God and the church. He was most interested in knowing when people started to have their own ideas about God, and he wanted to understand the changes that occurred in people's lives in regard to their belief in God. Then he asked seekers what they'd like to have as part of a spiritual environment. Harry and Chuck also looked at the generational differences in attitude toward God and the church. They were particularly interested in how the message and delivery strategy of the traditional church failed to reach seekers and which barriers kept people from seeking spiritual guidance from the church. Finally, they examined the challenges they would face in trying to attract people to spiritual worship while maintaining a certain distance and autonomy from the traditional idea of church. The information they funneled from all their research went into the design of the earliest prototype services. These services were important in measuring the interest in and attraction and response to the design of a seeker service.

Harry and Chuck, along with the ministry team, also had countless conversations and retreats about the spiritual principles Journeys Community would embody. Their theology, they decided, would be one of conscious consideration for all spiritual paths. Their message would be based on individual experience, and they would refrain from espousing a particular theological or religious view and allow seekers to find their own meaning in each service. They would use popular culture, not just traditional texts, to explore their spirituality. There were disagreements about the content, tone, and purpose of Journeys Community, and some ministry team members left and others joined. Eventually, a team of eight was assembled. Four prototype services later, the team began planning weekly services.

A Work in Progress

With each success and small step forward, Harry and the ministry team realized there was still more for them to learn. Forming a seeker community also involves the process of developing support. For Journeys Community, this included everything from looking for an appropriate venue for hosting services, to establishing a corporate structure and status as a nonprofit entity, to securing insurance and legal rights for the copyrighted materials they used. It also required the team to solicit financial backing, find musicians and technical equipment, advertise, and develop a regular following of seekers who participated weekly. Though the business and operational side of starting a seeker community is less exciting than the creative process of designing spiritual services, it requires just as much time and effort to be successful.

The following chapters describe how to recruit a ministry team and create prototype services, as well as how to develop support, generate interest, and publicize Journeys Community to a growing but geographically disparate groups of seekers. Since there was no model for Journeys Community to follow as the team members worked to create a seeker ministry, this book is based on their experience and can serve as a guide to other individuals, organizations, and institutions that are interested in forming a seeker community of their own.

CHAPTER 4

RECRUITING
A MINISTRY TEAM

The most important aspect of creating a seeker community is finding the right ministry team. One of the biggest challenges Harry faced in creating Journeys Community was recruiting a team who understood his vision. Journeys Community couldn't have been formed—or been as successful as it is—without ministry team members who fully agreed with the purpose and function of a seeker community.

Though there are many religious leaders who feel it's important to reach out to seekers, there aren't nearly as many who understand seekers' spiritual needs—consider those Christians who refer to seekers as "the lost." Assuming that seekers are "lost" misunderstands the spiritual needs of people who've found the church unfulfilling. Many churches create seeker communities in the hope of eventually transforming people from seekers to church members. These seeker ministries merely serve as contemporary stepping-stones to the larger church. Many "Christian seeker ministries" created as annexes of the larger church haven't experienced long-term success simply because there is an expectation and goal for what the seeker should become. The seeker community is seen by church leaders and members as a means to an end. It is a process of trying to make seekers become like them, and because of that, they have failed in significant ways to reach seekers at their core.

Harry, in recruiting his ministry team, insisted that team members not think of a seeker community as a back door to the traditional church. Despite advice warning him that seeker communities fail unless they have Christ and Christian teachings at their core, Harry realized that true seekers need a community of their own, a place to safely worship the God of their own understanding. There could be no ulterior motive in forming the community. This is the most essential concept in creating a seeker community and a significant departure from traditional Christian thinking about evangelism.

Along the way, Harry attracted some church members who were interested for a time in being a part of Journeys Community, but they eventually left because they had difficulty letting go of the notion that "the lost" should be encouraged to join "believers" in order to find spiritual salvation. A husband and wife team of musicians, Hal and Joy, were very active in the early formation of Journeys Community and helped Harry shape some of the first prototype services. However, Joy eventually left the ministry team because she felt the goal of the seeker community should be to bring people to Christ. Hal soon followed, unable to split his attention, time, and commitment between his former congregation and the seeker community that was being formed. At another point, Harry met an enthusiastic young man named John who was interested in helping with the technical aspects of Journeys Community services. But he too left quickly because he misunderstood the purpose of a seeker community and felt more at home in his traditional congregation. Harry also met George, a church leader. Though it was never his intention to leave the traditional church, George lent his support but was afraid that seekers would be more interested in self-help than in spirituality. His opinion of what motivates seekers is not uncommon among church leaders. Many church leaders fear that psychology has replaced religion in this postmodern society. Had George remained a member of the Journeys Community ministry team, he would have been greatly surprised by the deep and rich spiritual lives of its members. In all four cases, Hal, Joy, John, and George weren't suited to join a seeker ministry team because they either misunderstood the purpose of a seeker community, were interested in directing seekers toward a particular dogma, were unable to commit the time and effort necessary to build a community, or were fulfilled by their own religious practice and felt no need to expand.

Some church members are interested in presenting the gospel in contemporary and creative ways to spiritual seekers who haven't yet found salvation in Christ. Their misunderstanding of a seeker community as a contemporary means of spreading the gospel is the view that most church members hold when they attempt to reach out to seekers. However, it is important to emphasize that in order to build a true seeker community, there must be no expectation or requirement for what seekers should believe or how they should worship. The purpose of a seeker community is to allow people to explore their own spiritual paths in the company of others who are on a similar journey. The only expectation that Journeys Community carries is the hope that, as seekers, we will be able to deepen our spiritual lives in ways that are beneficial to us and others.

Recruiting Seekers to Join a Ministry Team

Early members of the Journeys Community came from a variety of backgrounds. Some were church members seeking to expand their spirituality beyond the traditional teachings of the church. Some, like Valerie, were intrigued by Harry's enthusiasm and vision for Journeys Community. A longtime member of Harry's former Episcopal congregation, she became an early member of the Journeys ministry team. She says:

> The conservative vestry was as reluctant to support this new ministry as they were fond of Harry and aware of its importance to him. As I listened to him repeatedly have to justify his expenditure of time and energy on this project, I realized that this ministry was where my heart and head wanted to be. So I volunteered to be the liaison person between the vestry and the seeker ministry.

As a seeker, Val is an avid reader of spiritual texts from all traditions and is curious about the process of discovering God in all of life. Although she was baptized in the Episcopal Church, she says, "Once I linked up with the core development team, the pull was immediate and total."

Another seeker from Harry's previous ministry was Barbara, who, like Valerie, joined the ministry team early on. Barbara was a longtime friend of Harry's with whom he shared his early interest in contemporary spirituality. In her career as a scientist, Barbara discovered the limits of science to explain the mysteries of life. Her reading of *The Celestine Prophecy*[1] started her on her spiritual journey. Her growing appreciation of the spiritual nature of all life has made her a valuable member of the Journeys Community ministry team.

Harry met Paul while they were both active in traditional congregations and invited him to become a member of the ministry team. The fact that Paul was also an ordained minister with a career in pastoral counseling and psychology lent an open perspective to the ministry team. Along with his deep respect for the spirituality in all of life, Paul brought the gift of storytelling to the fledgling seeker community to dramatically illustrate the important themes. Along with Harry, he understood the inner workings of the church and wanted to be involved in an organization that was reaching out to seekers with an attitude of spiritual acceptance. He says, "Religion that isn't spiritual isn't particularly valuable. I would venture to say that one of the things a lot of people who are drawn to Journeys Community might have in common is a hunger for spirituality. Religion can be a highly beneficial route to the spiritual path, but for many, religion and the challenges surrounding it have not illuminated the spiritual path." On his spiritual journey, Paul has come to believe that spirituality permeates all of life. For him, spirituality has to do with accepting life with all its mystery and trusting that it is a good gift that fills life with meaning and purpose.

Those attracted to Harry's ministry, of course, were seekers themselves. They were relieved that there was no ministry goal to transform seekers. In fact, many would not have agreed to join the ministry team if there had been an unspoken intention of graduating seekers to the traditional church. The ministry team, in discussing the open-ended theology they would embrace, agreed that Journeys Community should be available to facilitate people on their spiritual paths, not to steer them in a particular direction.

Developing a Creative Team

The creative team, which consists of a creative director, musical director, and technical director, is responsible for brainstorming, researching, and producing weekly spiritual services that are contemporary and creative.

The prototype services that the ministry team designed and hosted proved to be a fruitful method of finding interested seekers to join the effort. Jennifer was invited to attend one of the early prototype services and give feedback as part of the feasibility study and marketing research that Chuck was conducting. She was impressed with the efforts the ministry team made to reach beyond the walls of the traditional church to be more inclusive in its message and method. In fact, the message of the service stayed with her well after she left the service and later inspired her to write a lengthy email to Chuck outlining ideas and songs and readings the team could use in designing future services. Jennifer was soon recruited for the position of creative director. She was drawn to Journeys

Community specifically because it wasn't a church. She'd had limited exposure to several Catholic and evangelical churches growing up, but in each case she had felt excluded, never fully believed church doctrine, and had a difficult time relating the biblical language to anything in her life. But she was attracted to Journeys Community because it allowed her to explore her own spiritual beliefs without being told what she should believe, and because it referred to itself as a spiritual community for people who were uninterested in church. Jennifer appreciated that.

Despite growing up in an agnostic household, Michele, a professional vocalist and mother, had always been curious about religion and spirituality. With each major turning point in her life, her desire to connect spiritually with others continued to grow. After reading about Journeys Community in a newspaper article, she attended a service and Harry invited her to join the ministry team. She, along with a guitarist and a pianist, Dave and Patty, attract people back to Journeys Community week after week with musical diversity and emotional depth. Before meeting Michele, Harry had been searching for other musicians to join his team, but in each case, the musicians he interviewed were either limited in the range of styles they could perform, were unwilling to commit the time and effort to help design services as part of the ministry team, or did not embrace the vision of Journeys Community. As the musical director of Journeys Community, Michele attends ministry team meetings to brainstorm ideas around a particular theme; she researches songs to complement the theme, finds lyrics and music for the musicians to practice, then rehearses and performs the music each Sunday morning. Most of the music Michele and the other musicians perform is contemporary, but they've also included gospel, old spirituals, bluegrass tunes, Native American chants, classical music, and African drumming. The diversity of music keeps the services fresh and engaging.

The technical director, Steve, came to Journeys Community through an arts organization where Harry had advertised. Although religion was not part of his childhood, Steve had always been interested in a spiritual life and explored more than a few religious perspectives in his travels. He attended Catholic masses, converted to conservative Judaism, attended evangelical Christian services, and delved into Buddhism looking for a unified view that could get to the spiritual heart of life and help him reconnect with God. Steve joined the Journeys Community team to provide the technological know-how for the audio-visual part of the service, support the website, and produce a weekly newsletter. He designs a PowerPoint presentation for each service that combines quotes, readings, images, lyrics, and movie clips for each theme. In starting a seeker community, the right creative mix and the right talent are essential for the design and production of weekly services. Though several people assist in brainstorming and shaping spiritual themes, the creative director oversees the service as a whole while paying close attention to the individual parts. Not only does the creative director research contemporary readings, spiritual texts, quotes, movies, songs, and ideas, but she integrates these elements, artfully arranging them to illustrate a particular theme. She's also an architect of the service structure, making sure the emotional arc of the service corresponds with the topic. For instance, in designing a theme about the meditations of St. Ignatius, the creative director allows for a time of quiet contemplation. In a quiet service, the spiritual convergence—the point where community members personally interact with the theme—must reflect the need for prayer. In another service focusing more on community interaction—say, a service about the spiritual implications of joy and laughter in daily life—the creative director may incorporate a group discussion to allow people time to share their joy in community. Though the design team doesn't sculpt the message for each service, the creative director integrates all aspects of the service to serve the larger theme.

Together, the creative director, music director, and technical director, as the heart of the creative ministry team, need a wide range of knowledge of contemporary culture in all its artistic forms. This sense of creativity is at the heart of Journeys Community, and it is what attracts seekers back week after week. Community members never know if they will be participating in a Japanese tea ceremony, writing messages of hope onto Buddhist prayer flags, or enacting the Benedictine ceremony of forgiveness and reconciliation by scooping their hands into a bowl of water, then opening their palms to symbolically release the grievance. In designing these diverse services, the ministry team adheres to a common denominator: we must personally connect with the theme and like the music, readings, and other content we contribute to the service. A song with perfect lyrics but an unappealing melody isn't used. The litmus test for all content is whether or not the particular piece touches the heart. The ministry team has found that if a service appeals to the heart rather than the intellect, there will be a greater chance of connecting to the Divine.

At Journeys Community it is understood that seekers follow their own paths no matter where they lead—or don't lead. Because of this open approach, a few spiritual seekers who have participated in Journeys Community have reconciled themselves with their childhood religion and returned to the traditional church with a fresh perspective. Others, with no intention of returning to church, have made peace with the deeply held misgivings about traditional religion. One member, who remains very active in Journeys Community, has started attending evening vespers at a local Episcopal church. The open and accepting environment at Journeys Community has enabled seekers to feel safe in spiritual exploration and no longer isolated in their beliefs.

If church leaders are concerned about the prospect of facilitating self-help groups rather than helping people explore the rich terrain of their spiritual lives, they can rest easy. The depth and diversity of spiritual experiences among community members are both refreshing and engaging. In fact, in the beginning stages of Journeys Community, if there had been an unstated agenda that the ministry team would provide knowledge to seekers in need of spiritual teaching, this unwitting arrogance would have disappeared quickly when the people attending Journeys Community proved to have deep spiritual knowledge of their own. The extent to which some have sought to enrich their own spiritual lives outside of the church was a welcome surprise and a joy for Harry to witness. Instead of people waiting to be fed spiritual knowledge on Sunday morning, as in many traditional churches, Harry discovered that the seekers who participate in Journeys Community have great spiritual richness and experience to contribute. Steve's experience at Journeys Community, not only as a team member but as a seeker, is a rich example of community members learning from one another.

• STEVE'S STORY •

I joined Journeys Community as the technical director for reasons other than spiritual or social connection. I came to the group as a way to make some extra money while doing something interesting and creative.

When I first joined I expected only to do my job. I had a life story with its share of sacred and profane experiences. I felt like I had a good understanding of myself and my place in the world. With intense self-examination and questioning, I had come through a turbulent and difficult period in my life. I felt like I had survived. In some ways, I felt like I was done with exploring the inner life. I soon learned otherwise.

Being a member of the ministry team, I don't always have the chance to experience the services on Sunday through the same eyes as the community members. My Sunday happens when our team meets during the week to plan the services. Much of the work we do is planning and organizing the service, but this practical work is driven by spiritual work. The spiritual work happens when each of us brings our own experiences to the table. We share our perspectives and knowledge. We share our stories. We share our lives. We ask each other questions, and we challenge each other to go deeper so that the services and content we bring on Sunday have meaning to the community. This process means so much to me. I have learned more about myself and my connection to God than I had learned in all the years before coming to Journeys. Through working on this team and creating these services, I have found a deeper connection to God. I have a better sense of what is important in life and how to be a better human being. The people on this team have been so essential to this.

Perhaps the biggest surprise to members of the ministry team is the amount of spiritual nourishment we've received and been able to give each other. This wasn't something Harry anticipated when he and Chuck began their planning, but it seems to be the natural result of people helping each other in their search for God. The fact that many of us are deepening our spiritual lives outside the traditional church is no cause for worry. In fact, as Chuck sees it, the whole world is benefited when more and more people seek out the God of their own understanding. The benefits are exponential.

Recruiting a Ministry Team

- Talk with several people, especially friends; soon enough those who understand your vision will ask to join you.

- Invite seekers to join you who will understand better than you do what they want out of a seeker community.

- Solicit interest from church members who are eager to expand their own spirituality beyond traditional religious teachings.

- Meet with clergy who've had experience with several traditions and who openly promote an acceptance of and tolerance toward all spiritual beliefs.

- Talk with creative people—musicians, artists, and writers—who understand your vision and will be filled with great ideas for you.

- Find people willing to commit the time and effort necessary to building a new community.

- Steer away from people who insist on a particular direction or dogma for your new community.

- Most important, be clear that you and your team don't have any ulterior motives in forming a seeker community and that you don't expect seekers to eventually become church members or Christian in their beliefs.

CHAPTER 5

DESIGNING PROTOTYPE SERVICES

The first task of the newly assembled ministry team was to design a prototype service. In the span of a year, the team designed and hosted four prototype services that served as trial balloons for what would later become Journeys Community. These early prototypes had several functions: they provided a training ground for the ministry team; they allowed us to gain feedback from participants; and they alerted and attracted seekers in the area to the new spiritual community that was being formed. The early prototype services were instrumental in launching Journeys Community into a weekly venture that has grown steadily over the past five years. But the prototypes were just the beginning step in a learning process that continues to evolve. There was so much more the ministry team needed to discover that could only be learned through the process of creating services week after week.

The Early Prototypes

Chuck and Harry met for months to discuss what they perceived to be the key elements of a seeker service, basing their ideas on information they gathered from personal interviews and phone surveys that Chuck conducted with seekers. He recorded the spiritual biographies of several people to understand the interests and needs of seekers; he also tallied the results of a phone survey of a particular geographical area to determine the potential interest in a new spiritual community. Finally, it was time for action. Following the process of product design in business, the team developed a service, invited a sampling of people to attend, and created a focus group afterwards. The first prototype service led them further into the process of discovery so that in a year's time, they'd planned three more prototype services and felt confident enough to begin designing services weekly. But hosting these prototype services was an important step for the ministry team in learning how to design services that would attract and engage seekers.

Since, as a ministry team, we are seekers ourselves, we chose topics that interested us and furthered our own spiritual paths. The first service was designed around the theme "Orphanhood," which touched on Harry's personal story and experience and expanded to address the universal feelings of loneliness and isolation that all of us have felt at one time or another. It included a film clip from the movie *Cider House Rules*, which proved to be very effective in eliciting emotion. The second prototype, "When the Stranger at the Door is God," took a contemporary look at the Benedictine rule to treat every stranger at the door as God. It included a passage written by Buddhist monk Thich Naht Hanh and a song by Joan Osborn, "What If God Was One of Us?" both of which underscored the theme. The seekers who participated enjoyed the multi-denominational approach of this service. The third prototype service, "The Spiritual Journey," included a reading from the book *Oh, the Places You'll Go!* by Dr. Seuss. The fourth service, hosted on Father's Day, examined the question, "Who is my father?" to explore in a deeper way our relationships with others and with God.

Immediately after each prototype service, Chuck gathered suggestions and criticisms from a focus group in regard to the format, the content, and the emotional and spiritual connection. The ministry team used this feedback to make calculated decisions about how to improve the design, content, and flow of a seeker service. Perhaps the most important lesson the ministry team learned from the prototype services was about the manner in which the spiritual reflection was delivered. As Chuck remembers it, "We realized right off the bat that having a central figure as the leader and everyone else in the audience as separate and apart was problematic. That did *not* work. In some ways, the prototypes were not very good at all because they were didactic." So we had to learn how to eliminate the barriers between the ministry team who was creating the services and the audience whom we were asking to participate. We also recognized how important it is not to preach to the audience. Instead, we practiced speaking about our own experience in a way that was personal and revealing. We were very clear about not wanting to give prescribed answers to the people who participated in our services and felt is was essential to talk about our own spiritual experience rather than give our opinions. Our job as a design team was to present movie clips, songs, personal stories, and readings and let seekers discover the meaning for themselves.

We also needed to answer several other basic questions in order to create services that flowed more freely. So we asked the focus groups and ourselves, as seekers, what worked best. We had specific questions about design, content, and message that, in some cases, were answered by trial and error.

We Asked about Format and Design

- Should the ministry team introduce and explain each theme at the beginning of the service or let seekers determine it for themselves?
- Where and how should we add prayer in the service?
- What should be the metaphor for the spiritual meal?

We Asked about Content

- Do we need to include more images?
- Were recorded songs as effective as live performances?
- Were the readings we chose too long?
- Were the film clips we chose long enough?
- Did the services have an emotional heart? Were they uplifting?

We Asked about the Spiritual Message

- How long can the spiritual leader's reflection be before seekers lose interest?
- How can spiritual leaders present their reflections so they sound fresh and engaging and not prescriptive or like a sermon in church?
- How should spiritual leaders introduce and end group discussions?
- How would seekers feel about sharing their experiences freely in group discussions?

Designing Weekly Services

The prototype services answered some questions and solved some problems for the design team. Our answers came through trial and error, but in the beginning, we had to guess based on our own preferences and experiences as seekers ourselves. Though the initial planning for the prototype services took months, the team quickly fell into a pace of simultaneously designing several services weeks in advance of the actual services. It is important to note the significance of planning services in advance: often our ideas and emotional responses to a theme will occur a week or two after our initial discussion. Only in this way are we sure to understand the emotional depth of what we are creating. This is a key point for any ministry team to recognize. Unfortunately, this process of developing themes over a period of time is rarely used in the traditional church, where services may not be as deeply or as carefully thought through. As part of our long-term planning process, the team continues to meet once a week for two hours, occasionally adding another meeting during the course of a month to brainstorm future themes. Over time, a pattern for planning our services has emerged.

We Ask Essential Questions

In designing services each week, we immediately discovered two very important criteria that continue to be our guiding principles as we brainstorm and research themes. The first essential criterion in designing a service is the answer to the question, "Where is God in this?" Whether the theme is fear or hope or laughter, the ministry team needs to discuss the spiritual depth of each topic to make sure that the service has spiritual and emotional depth on Sunday. The team gathers for two hours each week to brainstorm new services and contemplate the spiritual reflection. We must be able to answer the question, "Where is God in this?" to be clear that each of us understands the direction of the services we're creating. Sometimes the question requires contemplation and discussion to avoid easy answers or a shallow understanding of God's presence. Seekers are questioners, so we on the ministry team must question ourselves as well in order to fully explore all aspects of a theme. In a service about peace, for example, we asked each other, "What is peace?" We became clear about whether we were designing a service to address inner peace in the midst of chaos or the external worldwide experience of peace. We meditated on these two views of peace and then asked ourselves, "How do we live peaceably with each other despite our different views on how to create peace?" And "What do you do when you are seeking peace and those around you are not?" Most important, we asked ourselves how God reveals God's presence through peace. Does the Divine, for example, create war and peace, or are God's love and peace always available to people? In our questioning, we may not come up with a definitive answer, nor is our aim to come up with a single response. We feel it is important to explore these questions in each service we design so that on Sunday mornings the depth of the service will allow seekers to form their own ideas and understanding.

We Make an Emotional Connection with the Content

The other essential criterion the team follows in designing each service is this: we must connect with the spiritual content we brainstorm and research. As a team, we must like the movie clip or music or reading for a service we're designing if it is to be a successful service. Our personal likes and dislikes are important in forming authentic services. As spiritual seekers, we are at times skeptical, questioning, and particular. One measure we use to gauge our connection with the content is to determine whether the content appeals more to the heart than the head. In our brainstorming sessions, we may come up with several suggestions for music and readings and movies; we may even find a song with lyrics that perfectly underscore the theme, but if one of us finds the melody of the song to be too sappy or dull, we scrap the song from the service in favor of something that has more heart and melody. In fact, we team members often hear the musical suggestions with our hearts, listening for the feeling of a song and its emotional impact. Likewise, we choose spiritual readings based on the spiritual and emotional impact rather than the intellectual understanding of a theme. We've found that if we choose content that isn't moving or exciting to us, our services will be flat and ineffectual.

We Present the Theme

As we began to create weekly services, the answers to some of the questions we wrestled with in the early prototype services became clear, sometimes through serendipitous successes and sometimes through experimentation. An initial question we pondered had to do with the amount of introduction and explanation the spiritual leader should give at the beginning of each service. We were aware that we wanted seekers to determine their own meaning, yet the ministry team didn't want to leave participants directionless and confused. How much introduction is too much? Or how little is not enough? Through experience and feedback, we discovered that, depending on the theme, some services should begin with a brief introduction to give seekers an understanding of the direction the service will follow. Other services are more straightforward with a theme that is easily identified, so an explanation isn't needed. For instance, a service on the meditations of St. Ignatius requires an introduction so the community will understand the format of the meditations; on the other hand, a service on forgiveness that begins with a powerful film clip needs no explanation or introduction. Often suggestions from community members have helped us in this process and continue to inform us of what works.

We Include Prayer

The question of prayer, how and where to include it, was another element of design the team wanted to understand. Our concern in creating Journeys Community was that, as an alternative to church, it be as unlike church as possible. Because seekers have been unfulfilled or turned off by the traditional church, it was important for the design team to create spiritual depth without emulating the ritual and rote prayer of church. At the same time, we understood the importance of including prayer in our format. For some people, the period of silent meditation is a time for prayer. For others, the meditation itself *is* prayer, where people can listen for the voice of God within, which is, to them, more authentic than reciting the words of a prayer. We found through experience that, depending on the theme, a prayer said together as a community is most effective near the end of the service, either before or after the spiritual meal, to add depth and meaning to the theme. The fact that the prayer is said as a community gives it more power as it connects us, through words, to the theme, each other, and the Divine.

We Incorporate a Spiritual Meal

The inclusion of a spiritual meal, like prayer, is important in creating meaning. In the early planning stages, the ministry team thought of the spiritual meal as a "eucharist," using traditional church language to describe it. But one of the most important things we discovered through the prototype services and focus groups was that the symbol of the "eucharist" needed to be replaced by the more universal and adaptable idea of a meal. This is a significant change that separates Journeys Community from the more narrow and confining emotional connection to the church and Christian theology. As a result, the spiritual meal has greater impact, metaphorical meaning, and intention. The meal itself changes from week to week, and its meaning depends on the theme. For instance, a meal for a service about taking time to pray and meditate can be a cup of chamomile tea to symbolize our willingness to silently drink in God; or a spiritual meal can be apples and honey to symbolize the spiritual sweetness of life. This changing symbolism is something the community celebrates and enjoys.

We Choose Music, Movies, Images, and Readings

We also had several questions about the presentation of the music, movies, images, and readings. Because we were creating the format for Journeys Community from week to week and using technology to project images, movie clips, and song lyrics on a screen at the front of the room, our initial impulse was to include as much content as we could present within an hour. But we soon realized we weren't giving the community members enough time to digest and meditate on the theme. Our early services were too full; the spiritual experience was crowded by sensory overload. As part of our constant experimentation and readjustment, we discovered that some of the readings we'd chosen were too long, too prescriptive, or too heady. So we changed our approach. Now most of the readings are short and heartfelt, such as Rumi's poems about awakening to the love of God. Once in a while the team will include a longer dramatic reading that is part of a story, such as an excerpt from Mark Twain's story "The Private History of a Campaign That Failed," based on his own experiences in war. Journeys Community used this narrative in a service designed around the search for God in the midst of war. In the absence of a movie clip, a dramatic narrative can move the community into a deep emotional place.

The temptation to use many images throughout a service also had mixed results. Sometimes images can provide a visual aid in discussing a theme; they can show something profound with their silence that might be too difficult to explain in words. In a service on impermanence, we found a series of photographs by artist Andy Goldsworthy showing a snow-covered tree in winter in various stages of thaw until the same tree is photographed in spring, covered in dandelions. These photographs were meditations on the cycles of life and nature, profound in their beauty and simplicity. At other times, we've gathered photographs from the com-

munity and flashed family pictures on the screen to illustrate our connection to each other and to our families. But we've also found that too many
images can be distracting. For instance, projecting images on the screen
during the performance of a song in an attempt to create a sort of music
video montage actually interfered with the sense of meditation that was
needed. Now we project most of our images, interspersed with quotations, at the beginning of the service when community members are
arriving and can reflect on them. A single image is also used to introduce
the silent meditation each week. The image is meant to be introspective,
offering seekers a way into the quiet.

We Decide How Much Is Too Much

Another important realization about images and technology was this:
even though too many images can be distracting, film clips are ineffective
if they are too short. Film clips that are under three minutes long feel
rushed and random; they don't leave enough time for the dramatic ten-
sion to captivate the community. There must be a period of adjustment
and build-up so participants can immerse themselves in the story of the
film in order to fully feel its impact. Most film clips we use are between
four and seven minutes long. Clips exceeding seven minutes, unless
they're full of action, start to feel lengthy and tend to drag out the point.
Video montages, interviews, and documentaries are exceptions to the
three-minute rule. When the design team found a documentary by Bill
Moyers on the song "Amazing Grace," we were able to extract a small clip
to great effect. To decide on a film clip's length and potential power, we
listen and watch with our hearts rather than our heads. We rely on our
emotional response to a film clip, and if we feel it doesn't move us to a
deeper understanding, we don't use it. Sometimes, if a particular film has
more than one relevant clip, the technical director edits sections of a
movie together or else we show the sections at different times during the
service. For instance, when we used the movie *Groundhog Day*, we showed
three different clips of the film at various points in the service to emphasize the theme and the character's transformation at the end.

We Choose Live or Recorded Music

We've also experimented with recorded music versus live music. Not surprisingly, live music is usually more effective at reaching the emotional
depth seekers crave. The musicians at Journeys Community are proficient
in a wide range of musical genres. In a single service, they might play

gospel, classical, and pop music. Only on rare occasions do they play recorded music if a particular song is deeply moving but too difficult to perform live with the same effect. However, there are certain points in a service when a meditative or ethereal effect is needed that can only be provided by recorded music. Usually, the team plays recorded music at the beginning of a service when community members are arriving and later when the spiritual meal is being served. We change our musical selection from week to week, trying to match our music selection to the theme. The recorded music at the beginning of a service could be classical piano, nature sounds, Gregorian chants, Japanese melodies, electronic pop, or instrumental movie soundtracks. The recorded music adds texture and mood to the weekly services.

We Discover the Emotional Heart of the Service

With time, the design team has come to recognize that each service has an emotional heart—the point in the service that becomes the spiritual center because it's most moving and experiential. It may change from week to week. Sometimes the heart of a service centers around the reflection and personal story given by the spiritual leader; other times the drama of a particular film clip is the most moving element of the service. In designing each service, we're clear that we're not in the business of orchestrating "experiences" and manipulating emotions to reach a phony spiritual climax. Instead, we choose content that moves us and makes us mindful of our own spiritual paths. We brainstorm ideas each week in the hope that community members will respond, but our task isn't to steer members into a prescribed spiritual understanding. The emotion that many people experience week after week is as much a result of their own willingness to open themselves to the God of their own understanding as it is of the format and content provided by the design team. Often the team is astounded by the positive response to a particular element of the service. It's this authentic experience of God in our midst that seekers have been coming back for week after week.

Sharing a Spiritual Message

At Journeys Community, the person who assumes the role of spiritual leader changes from week to week. The team decided in the early planning stages that the role of spiritual leader should be a rotating position because we wanted to acknowledge the Divine in each of us—none of us is closer to God and spirituality than any other. There is no special requirement to be the spiritual leader except a desire to share one's personal experience about a particular theme. This egalitarian approach has proved refreshing to the seeker community. This multiplicity of voices and experiences not only gives access to many views of the spiritual experience, but also recognizes that each of us has something of God to share. It affirms the seeker's individual path and beliefs by allowing room for many interpretations of the spiritual experience. Following are some of the guidelines we've developed for the spiritual message.

We Speak in the First Person

In the early days of creating prototype services, the ministry team was adamant about the importance of sharing personal stories rather than opinions in our reflections about the nature of God and spirituality. Since the beginning of time, stories have been an essential way for us to gain entry to our inner lives and to recognize ourselves in relation to the rest of the world. Storytelling is also important because it assumes a different tone and stance than does preaching. It offers an authenticity and an emotion that are impossible to deny. The team understood that personal stories provide a means for us to relate to one another, and we were determined to tie the spiritual reflection to personal experience. Spiritual leaders might be drawn to a particular theme based on a desire to speak to the theme and explore their own questions and spiritual experiences. Harry, for instance, had a personal stake in talking about an orphanhood of the spirit because he was intimate with the subject. Chuck was drawn toward creating a service exploring the life of St. Teresa of Avila because he had studied her life for several years. In many instances, we've listened to or read each other's spiritual reflections at the weekly brainstorming meetings to ensure that enough emotional and personal experiences are being relayed. We listen for the personal experience of a theme and point out the abstractions or heady ideas that may be intellectually interesting but not heartfelt.

We've also found that speaking in the first person is essential in making seekers feel comfortable. Everyone has a message to share, and none of us has an exclusive ear to God, so when spiritual leaders speak in the first person to relate their own experiences, seekers can respect the message without feeling as though they must abide by it. Relating our own experience of the Divine in the first person offers seekers the opportunity to accept or reject any part of the reflection; they have the freedom to decide what works for them on their spiritual paths without feeling as though their personal beliefs are being threatened. They are free to take what is helpful and disregard the rest. The point is for the spiritual leader at Journeys Community to sound less like a preacher and more like an ordinary person who is traveling his or her own spiritual path.

We Limit Our Talks to Fifteen Minutes

Just as personal experience is important in creating a spiritual message for seekers who don't want to be preached at, the length of the reflection is important too. Seekers have a limited tolerance for listening to just one person's point of view. That's why most reflections at Journeys Community last about fifteen minutes or less. The team knows that if a reflection goes on too long, it begins to sound like preaching, and seekers are highly sensitive to and wary of being preached at. The spiritual reflection may be divided into two parts and given by two leaders who share their divergent or complementary experiences related to the theme. Some services are leaderless; the ministry team allows the message to come through the music, videos, readings, and meditations they've chosen, allowing community members to find their own meaning. The approach of leaderless services has worked well with topics that are more abstract—contemplating faith, for instance—because the question of faith with seekers is such an individual matter.

We Use the Format of Group Discussion

Group discussions are another way of opening the spiritual reflection to the larger collective experience of the group. The early ministry team knew that allowing seekers a voice as part of the service by creating group discussions was a significant departure from the traditional church. But they were certain that seekers had much of their own lives to share even if they didn't recognize it. In planning services that included time for group discussion in their format, the team members had a couple of questions. To begin with, they wondered how the spiritual leader could successfully open a theme to a deeper discussion. They wanted the discussions to be lively, not flat. They also wanted to encourage seekers to share something of their personal experience rather than abstract ideas or theories. But they weren't sure how safe and uninhibited people would feel sharing in a large group. So the team also considered the possibility of creating smaller discussion groups that were meant to foster a sense of security and intimacy.

Finding the right questions. The answers to these questions came through practice. In the early days of Journeys Community, the team had not yet learned how important it is to ask specific questions in order to gain a lively response in a group discussion. We discovered that some questions are too vague and result in a lot of silence during the discussion. We soon realized that the questions we pose to the community have to be stimulating enough to tap into personal experience. They also have to be grounded in the spiritual leader's own experience. During the planning sessions, members of the design team ask each other the questions we intend to ask during the service. We ask the questions of ourselves to ensure that what we are asking is probing, direct, and easy to relate to. If we have trouble answering our own questions, we know we must find another way to ask. As with everything else, we adhere to the "heart versus head" rule. If a question we plan to ask doesn't penetrate deeply enough below the intellect, then we know we have to redesign the question. Suppose, for example, we plan a group discussion about the meaning of prayer. Unsuccessful abstract questions might include the following:

- "What does prayer mean to you in your life?"
- "How has prayer helped you on your journey?"

These questions require some thought, which isn't bad in itself, but they don't offer ready responses. Here are examples of better questions to ask that encourage us to think about our experiences with the meaning of prayer:

- "What are some of the ways that you practice prayer in your life?"
- "Do you recall an event in your life when prayer was particularly meaningful?"

Questions that tap into personal experience lead to group discussions that are both heartfelt and practical. We can listen to each other's experience and glean useful suggestions about new ways to incorporate the Spirit of God into our daily lives.

Waiting for answers. Another important lesson the team learned in leading group discussions was the patience of waiting. A theme or a question may require a bit of reflection before the community will share. The spiritual leaders have had to force themselves to wait through a bit of anxious silence until someone is willing to respond. Usually, the waiting feels longer to the spiritual leader holding the microphone at the front of the room than it does to the rest of the community. Nevertheless, it's important that the spiritual leader overcome the temptation to end the group discussion early. Sooner or later community members speak up. Often, it just takes one or two volunteers to get the ball rolling. After a period of silence, someone's comment might trigger a response in others who then share their own experience in relation to the theme. This problem of waiting, however, is minimal, and as the community grows and more people attend the services, there is less hesitation and silence during the group discussions.

To the delight of the ministry team, seekers have been eager to share their experiences. Originally the design team created periods of small-group discussions in which four or five community members would share their experiences as an alternative to speaking in front of a larger group. There was a fear that people would feel uncomfortable sharing their personal stories with the whole community. But the design team realized two things almost simultaneously: that smaller groups at times forced an intimacy that made some people shier in their willingness to share, and that the community as a whole missed out on the wisdom and experience of everyone else when it limited the size of the group discussions. Most seekers craved the larger group discussions, both the experience of listening and the experience of sharing. In fact, if there had been any sense of uncertainty about opening the floor to the uncensored remarks of the community—a fear that many traditional churches have—that hesitancy would have disappeared immediately. People respond enthusiastically to the prospect of being asked about their own lives and relationships to God. In many cases, the group discussion at Journeys Community is the only opportunity seekers have to share aloud about their deepest spiritual thoughts and experiences.

As the community grows, more time is built into the format of the service for group discussion. Usually the discussions last between ten and twenty minutes depending on the number of responses. The group discussions have become so popular that Journeys Community has formed a biweekly discussion meeting where community members can join together and discuss in greater depth the previous week's theme.

Sometimes the group discussion is the centerpiece of the service. To honor the need to give thanks at a Thanksgiving service, for instance, most of the hour was spent circling the room several times as community members shared what they were most grateful for in their lives. With each pass around the room, seekers offered deeper and richer expressions of their thanks to God. Often, the ministry team has found that the emotional heart of a service comes from the community members themselves during a time of discussion. The discussions complement and give depth and meaning to the spiritual reflection. They embrace the theology that each of us has something of the Divine within us to share. Though group discussions are not built into the format of every service, they are included often to connect community members with the theme and with each other. Through these discussions, the ministry team has discovered the rich spiritual depth that seekers bring with them on Sunday mornings and are so willing to share. Not surprisingly, it is the sharing of personal experience that unites the community.

CHAPTER 6

SECURING SUPPORT

After hosting four prototype services and making the decision to go forward with weekly services, the ministry team had to take important steps in developing Journeys Community as a legitimate organization. The business of establishing a seeker community entailed looking for an appropriate venue to host weekly services, finding and securing financial support, hiring part-time personnel, and creating a legal structure for the organization and its services. Harry's experience with organizational development was a guiding force in this process. Though less exciting and creative than designing weekly services, these steps were essential in establishing a firm foundation for Journeys Community.

Where to Meet

The ministry team was excited by the prospect of gathering regularly, but the question of where to meet required consideration. There were questions about the optimal location, affordability, and function of a building, all of which are important to address when trying to attract seekers to a new community. There were also practical requirements that had to be met in order for our services to be successful. We discussed our particular needs for a suitable space.

An adjustable space, with a screen and flexible seating. We knew that the interior setting of any space we used would have to be adjustable, since we'd need to set up and take down the props for our service every week. We also needed a space that had a screen at the front of the room,

since images and videos are an integral part of our services. Finally, we required flexible seating to accommodate the changing format of our services from week to week. To a degree, these requirements limited us in our search for a space.

Easy access. Accessibility was another important criterion. Journeys Community would be attracting an audience from a wide geographic area, so it was important to find a location that was close to major highways and near recognizable landmarks. Journeys Community had to be easy to find and convenient to many areas. The directions to Journeys Community needed to be simple to follow with clearly marked signs. Signage from the parking lot to the meeting space was important too. The point was to make finding Journeys Community as effortless as possible.

No church affiliation. The ministry team also understood, based on our research, that the meeting space we decided on couldn't be directly affiliated with any church. Many seekers have had negative experiences with the traditional church and, as a consequence, are wary of joining spiritual communities if they suspect or perceive a hidden agenda. The team members learned this lesson from the first prototype service, which had been hosted in a contemporary church. The response from the focus groups strongly recommended that future seeker services be divorced from a church setting. The focus group agreed that the prototype service had been stimulating, but it was impossible to ignore the altar and crucifix at the front of the room. As seekers, we're particularly sensitive to anything religious that suggests the service we are participating in is actually a "front" for an evangelizing effort. So the ministry team made sure the architecture and setting of the buildings we considered were free of religious overtones and symbols. We were careful about choosing a neutral location that wouldn't put off seekers from attending services.

Hospitable interior design. The ministry team had to address other issues of space as well, including the design of the interior where the services would be held. The ministry team wanted to create a warm and welcoming place for seekers, but for reasons more practical than the appearance of a space, we were limited in our search. Most important, we knew we needed a video screen that could be raised and lowered with ease. The screen would be a functional part of every service, basic to the design of each theme. In our search, we found plenty of rooms that offered a stage and screen, but many of these venues were set up as auditoriums with fixed stadium seats. But fixed seating is counter to creating a seeker community. Attached seats aren't warm or welcoming and limit personal involvement.

Fixed seats give a person the impression of being a detached member of an audience rather than an involved participant in an experience.

Among the spaces considered were meeting rooms and lounges on college campuses; performance spaces at arts-related venues and galleries; rooms in holistic and alternative medicine centers; recreation centers and community meeting spaces; theaters; schools; and senior centers. In some cases, the space was too large or too small, difficult to find, unavailable at certain times for prearranged functions (which would have meant canceling that week's service), inhospitable in appearance, or too expensive. Still, we narrowed the selection down to a handful of locations that seemed promising and eventually chose a local elementary school at which to host weekly services.

The first few years of Journeys Community were spent in the school cafeteria and auditorium. It offered us the flexibility to set up and take down our musical equipment and props week after week, plus the school had a screen built above the stage that could be easily raised and lowered. Though most auditoriums have fixed seating, this cafeteria/auditorium was designed for flexibility. Unfortunately, the concrete walls covered in construction paper and paintings of tropical fish lacked a sense of permanence. The members of the design team, with the help of community members, were able to find simple accessories that added a sense of spirituality and peace to the room. We covered a small piano bench with an embroidered cloth and placed a lamp on top, not to resemble an altar but to serve as a friendly place to rest the eye. We unrolled a small oriental rug in the front of the room to give warmth to the tile floor. And a community member donated an oriental screen, which we used to hide plugs and other technical equipment. The lighting was also an important element in creating atmosphere. The design team used the lamp on the bench as the only source of light, because the florescent overhead lights in the school were too bright and harsh for a spiritual setting. Though these adjustments to the space were relatively minor, they helped to transform the cafeteria into a more inviting place.

Eventually, Journeys Community moved from the school to its current location in a retirement community, which offered its auditorium at no charge. Not only is there a screen at the front of the stage, but the technical director has access to state-of-the art built-in audio and video equipment. The space is carpeted and beautifully decorated, with windows, adjustable lighting, and comfortable chairs that allow the flexibility to

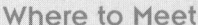

Where to Meet

- Find an adjustable multipurpose space with a screen and flexible seating.
- Make sure your location allows easy access from many locations.
- Chose a space that's free of any religious symbols or affiliations.
- Be sure the interior is neither too large nor too small but proportionate to the size of your group.
- Be creative in your chair arrangement week after week.
- Design a warm and welcoming atmosphere through lighting, rugs, flowers, and other props.

arrange the room and seating according to our needs each week. Usually, there are a few well-placed candles on the stage and a cloth-draped table off to the side that is wheeled to the front of the room for spiritual meals. This warm and professional setting has done much to boost attendance at Journeys Community services.

The comfortable and inviting arrangement of chairs is a weekly discussion topic among the ministry team. Straight rows would be too reminiscent of church pews or stadium seats, so we've experimented with semicircular rows, full circles, and small clusters, and we allow the arrangement to complement the weekly theme. Most often, the chairs are arranged in semicircular rows as a matter of convenience and inclusion, but at times we tighten the semicircle so that we almost face one another, providing a greater sense of intimacy and community during group discussions. We have also designed clusters of about five or six chairs gathered around a small platform of candles. For services on the spirituality of silence and meditation, these intimate clusters have been well received. In fact, the changing chair arrangement is something that community members look forward to. When the design team arranged the chairs one morning around small tables with cloths, teacups, and teapots, the community was excited in anticipation. The theme that morning was about how our daily rituals can be spiritual exercises; the spiritual convergence involved an adapted version of a Japanese tea ceremony to honor the holiness of everyday moments. The seating alone was instrumental in transforming the service into a memorable experience.

Securing Financial Support

Money, of course, is a principal concern in starting any venture, and this was no less true for starting Journeys Community. The Episcopal Church was instrumental in helping to develop and maintain a new seeker community, with no expectation that seekers should or would be funneled into the mainline church. This kind of support and encouragement with no strings attached was both gracious and vital to the early development of Journeys Community.

Outside funding is crucial for an initial six-to-nine-month period during which recruitment and planning take place for a new seeker community. After that, additional funding will be needed for the first three or four years of start-up operations, depending on how quickly the ministry grows. Sometimes the requirement of a sponsoring entity is that the fledgling organization be self-sufficient within a predetermined amount of time. It's been our experience that a newly organized seeker ministry can't be expected to be self-supporting until at least three years after it begins. A major part of the budget can be attained through in-kind services from a sponsoring organization. This includes the donation of a

Securing Financial Support

- Solicit support from a sponsoring organization or church.
- Make sure your financial gifts are free of any strings.
- Budget start-up money for an initial six-to-nine-month period.
- Continue to solicit funding from many sources for the first three or four years of operation.
- Attain support through in-kind services from other organizations.
- Research grants from local and national foundations.
- Cultivate relationships with individuals and organizations sympathetic to your cause.
- Encourage support from friends and community members.
- Be willing to operate on a shoestring budget with few paid employees.

meeting space and paid utilities, worship equipment and supplies, musicians and volunteers, umbrella insurance, hospitality supplies, office supplies, postage, and publicity.

Fortunately, the start-up costs of a seeker ministry are relatively minor compared to the operation costs of many churches. There are a couple of reasons for this. First, Journeys Community doesn't own a building or furnishings and has no expenses associated with maintaining such an enterprise. Nor do we pay our spiritual leaders, since this role is a rotating and shared position. Our operating costs are minimal. We pay the members of our creative team (the creative director, music director, and technical director) as part-time consultants, and the musicians are paid for each service in which they perform. We also own some basic technical and musical equipment, including a keyboard, a projector, and some microphones, though many of our assets have been donated. Finally, there is the cost of insurance, supplies, postage, and publicity. Our seeker community is a bare-bones operation that has been vastly successful in creating weekly services and engaging experiences for spiritual seekers. The traditional church could learn much from our model.

Harry, who has been our principal fundraiser, has found that financial support for a venture such as Journeys Community can come from a number of sources. First, a sponsoring organization—in our case, the Episcopal Diocese of Maryland—can be a generator of future contacts and financial resources. Often, the support lent by a sponsoring organization leads to grants and gifts from local and national church bodies. But grants from local and national foundations beyond the church and traditional religion are also important sources to research and pursue. In some cases, the grants might come with a particular stipulation, such as developing spiritual communities among young people. Journeys Community has benefited from such joint grants and associations and has expanded its efforts to reach young seekers at Goucher College.

With financial support from the Jessie Ball duPont Fund, Rev. Kelly Denton-Borhaug, the college's chaplain until July 2005, recruited a team of students to develop a program modeled on Journeys Community. They created a "Goucher Journeys" designed specifically for college students and hosted several exciting spiritual gatherings for their peers.

Researching grants and other support is an endless pursuit but is well worth the effort and time; it has allowed Journeys Community to forge relationships with unexpected allies who are greatly interested in the creative work we're doing. Finally, it's crucial to cultivate relationships with individuals and organizations. The encouragement and support of these close friends provide the foundation for becoming self-supporting.

The Legal Organization of Journeys Community

The legal and organizational issues involved in structuring a seeker community are important to address here. Journeys Community is incorporated as a 501(c)(3) nonprofit religious organization. Our nonprofit corporate status provides us with a separate legal and organizational identity and allows us to stand apart from our sponsor as a separate organization. This nonprofit corporate status also recognizes all donations made to Journeys Community as charitable contributions. Of course, a new seeker ministry needs to determine from the outset if it will be a separate entity from its sponsor. A group may decide that the new seeker community will be an outreach ministry of its sponsoring organization. In that case, no legal or corporate action needs to be taken. A word of caution about becoming an outreach ministry for another organization: this seeker ministry will have to work hard at maintaining a certain distance from its sponsor to attract seekers to a community that has no expectation for their spiritual direction. If a seeker community is too closely allied with another organization, especially a church, seekers will suspect this

Legal Notes

- Determine whether or not you'd like your seeker community to stand apart from its sponsoring church or organization— we recommend it.

- Structure your community to be a nonprofit religious organization in order to receive tax-exempt contributions.

- Acquire adequate insurance coverage.

- Establish copyright permission for movies, songs, and readings used in your services.

- Seek legal assistance to make sure all business issues are completely addressed.

new community is actually the traditional church in disguise. Based on many of their negative experiences in the past, seekers may be reluctant to join any group closely affiliated with the church. An outreach seeker ministry must be particularly careful about blurring the lines between itself and its parent organization.

If, on the other hand, a seeker ministry chooses to be organizationally and legally separate from its sponsor, if it has one, it must take specific protective actions. These include acquiring adequate insurance coverage to protect the corporate directors, the members of the ministry team, and the people who attend services, as well as establishing copyright permission for the right to show movie clips, perform songs, and use lyrics and other literary works. Permission for films can be gained for a yearly fee through Christian Copyright Licensing International (CCLI) and Christian Video Licensing International (CVLI); permission for literary works should be sought from the publisher. It's wise to seek legal assistance to ensure that all legal, corporate, and insurance issues are properly addressed.

Leadership

Addressing all the fundraising, rental, and legal issues takes time and effort, so one person should be designated to assume the role of organizer, coordinator, and leader, a position filled at Journeys Community by Harry. He's responsible for maintaining our ongoing relationship with the managers of the retirement facility; he also cultivates relationships within the community and establishes new contacts in his efforts to attract more seekers. A large part of his responsibility is procuring finan-

---

The Role of the Leader

- Assume the position of organizer, coordinator, and leader.
- Maintain relationships with other organizations and support services.
- Cultivate relationships within the community.
- Establish new contacts to attract seekers.
- Raise funds and procure financial support.
- Above all, be committed to the vision of a seeker community.

cial support for the community and dealing with legal and business issues. More than anything, the person who assumes this role needs to be committed to the vision of a seeker community and to be a seeker himself. It's also important that those who hold paid positions be fully committed to the vision of a seeker community. Without a committed ministry team of seekers devoted to their own spiritual growth, a seeker community won't succeed. Those of us on the ministry team must love what we do, enjoy the process of brainstorming and creating services week after week, and feel committed to the success of our organization. Though serving on the team is a part-time position, our dedication to the community is as much a dedication to ourselves and our own spiritual growth, a communal willingness to connect to the Divine and to one another.

CHAPTER 7

GETTING THE WORD OUT

One of the essential challenges of creating Journeys Community was *how to attract spiritual seekers—who were skeptical of religion—to a spiritual community designed specifically for them.*

The answer lies in the crafting of diverse and engaging services week after week, and because of that, Journeys Community has been successful in attracting a core group of committed members. Over the years our initial challenge has evolved into *how we can attract seekers to attend weekly Sunday services if they are not already in the habit of setting aside time for worship.*

We knew from our research that it would be difficult to persuade seekers to change their personal routines to attend spiritual services. We also knew that because seekers are independent in their thinking and beliefs, they're often skeptical about joining new groups. Many seekers are more comfortable with individual activities of spiritual expression, such as taking nature walks or walking a labyrinth, reading spiritual texts, journaling, practicing yoga, meditating, and watching spiritual films. When faced with the prospect of affiliating with a group, many seekers prefer to observe from the sidelines before joining. Even after agreeing to attend spiritual services, they may still be suspicious of any message that is remotely "religious" or proclaims to have "the answer." Seekers are repelled rather than drawn in by any attempts at evangelization. The ministry team at Journeys Community recognized these obstacles to building a seeker community from the beginning. That's why in trying to publicize Journeys Community, we've been mindful of how we present ourselves.

We knew that affiliating ourselves with other churches or ministries or even emulating their model of promotion wouldn't work for us. The concept of a multicultural spirituality based in contemporary music, movies, readings, and rituals is so new and different for most people—church people and seekers alike—that we had to develop our own unique identity, our own spiritual niche, our own publicity, and our own network of compatible groups and organizations with which to promote ourselves. As Chuck sees it, we need to talk about Journeys Community in a way that doesn't put seekers off and in a way that doesn't make us sound like a traditional church in disguise or a cult. The problem is that there is nothing else like Journeys Community with which to compare ourselves. Chuck says, "It's common sense, really: we tell our stories and play songs that are familiar and show movie clips as a way to deepen our spirituality."

The ministry team recognized that our style of advertising needed to have an attitude of attraction. Based on his experience with the traditional church, Chuck understood that no amount of promotion could foster a willingness in seekers to join an organization if they were not attracted to its message. In fact, churches have spent untold amounts of money trying to promote themselves to little avail. So we were faced with the task of advertising our spiritual community in a way that highlighted our sense of inclusion and individual belief. Seekers would need to be drawn to Journeys Community based on an attraction to the services we offered. Following are some of the strategies that have proved most effective for us.

Cultivating Relationships

Word of mouth. Not surprisingly, the best means of advertising is word of mouth. Many people, not just seekers, are hesitant about visiting a new group about which they're unsure. It's much easier to come with friends. Fortunately, seekers who attend our services have invited other friends and fellow seekers to join us; word of mouth has created a great network of relationships at Journeys Community. Most people who come to Journeys Community have been so enthralled by the services that they recognize they have a vested interest in supporting and continuing the community.

Hospitality. Members have organized a hospitality committee to greet newcomers. We understand that coming alone to a new group can be daunting. Newcomers often wonder, *Will I like it? Will it fit my beliefs? Will I feel welcome?* Some newcomers like to slip into the service unnoticed so they can leave if the service is not to their liking. The hospitality commit-

Getting the Word Out

- Cultivate relationships through word of mouth and invite friends.
- Organize a hospitality committee and greet newcomers.
- Design flyers and postcards to hand out and post.
- Invite spiritual workshop and retreat participants to attend.
- Create a weekly email newsletter.
- Affiliate with related groups and organizations.
- Advertise in weekly publications.
- Seek free publicity through news articles and human interest stories.
- Be willing to persevere.

tee has made a point of trying to welcome everyone and make them feel a part of the community while allowing them enough personal space to form their own opinions. Friendliness, a sense of inclusion, and openness go a long way in making seekers feel welcome. One community member, Janis, says, "I think that the welcome is the first impression someone has about the community, and if it's a warm one, they are more apt to feel good about their experience. It also provides a wonderful chance to introduce new people to the creative nature of the experience and perhaps describe a little bit about what to expect." Each week, the greeter has the opportunity to meet and connect with new people as well as regular attendees. Since the role of greeter is a rotating position, it's a great way for community members to get to know names and faces; name tags also have helped as Journeys Community has continued to grow.

Flyers and postcards. The enthusiasm and help from community members have been invaluable in other ways as well. In the first few months of Journeys Community, members volunteered to post flyers and announcements for Journeys Community at libraries and grocery stores and on community bulletin boards. Postcards are another easy way to advertise, since they are pocket-sized and easy to pass out. One couple who wanted to attract more seekers to our services even invited workshop and retreat participants whom they'd organized to join Journeys Community for an hour on Sunday morning before returning to their scheduled retreat. The commitment of community members to help ensure the success of Journeys Community has been one of the most effective means of attracting new seekers week after week. In fact, almost every week someone attends our service for the first time.

Newsletters and electronic media. To keep in touch and build a community in between services, a weekly email newsletter is sent out to everyone who signs up. This is both a means of getting the word out about Journeys Community and maintaining internal communications with our members. As much as possible, we try to include seekers by announcing the coming Sunday's spiritual theme the week before and by making the previous week's service content—readings, song lyrics, and spiritual reflection—available online for easy reference. Many people keep abreast of Journeys Community through our weekly newsletter and announcements though they live out of state. Some of these out-of-towners have either attended Journeys Community while visiting our area or found out about Journeys Community through friends and are intrigued and heartened by our services though they live too far away to attend. The website and the email list are maintained by the technical director and are useful tools in cultivating a community and keeping Journeys Community present and active in the lives of our members. As the number of people requesting the newsletter grows each week, the technical director has found an effective way of handling the traffic through a web-based management tool that allows for easy management of mass emails to members and provides attractive templates for newsletters and other announcements. This tool also allows community members and others to sign up to receive emails or change their address themselves, reducing the need to manage the email list manually and helping us meet legal requirements to make accessible opt-in and opt-out selections available to email recipients. The use of email has proved to be one of the best means for us to get the word out about our seeker community.

Networking. Through our community members we've also cultivated receptive and supportive affiliations with other groups and organizations. These networks include meditation groups, book clubs, film clubs that focus specifically on spiritual films, natural food devotees and health food stores, organizations concerned with holistic and alternative medicine, spiritual support groups, arts organizations, and many others. Through these affiliations we've been able to sponsor events—dances, talks, lectures, film screenings, and fundraising campaigns—to generate more interest in our community. Maintaining cooperative relationships with other groups and organizations with a similar spiritual focus has been an excellent way to attract new seekers to Journeys Community.

The press. In spreading the word about our community, we've also received a lot of attention from the press. We've actively sought and received publicity from the local and regional print media and local cable channels. We also advertise in weekly and monthly publications, listing the themes for upcoming services and briefly describing the creative nature of our services. These ads have been fruitful in drawing many new seekers in the area to our community; however, ads can be expensive. It is largely through articles and interviews that we've been able to reach a larger audience and paint a more complete picture of Journeys Community.

As part of our effort to attract seekers and publicize ourselves to the larger community, we've been the subject of feature stories in both secular and religious publications. Articles written about Journeys Community in the *Baltimore Sun* and the *Washington Post* focused on both the nature of a seeker ministry and interviews with ministry team members. We've also had write-ups that profiled our seeker ministry in a series of articles. Usually, interviewers are in search of a "hook," a unique way to look at the subject of faith. What makes Journeys Community so appealing to journalists is our multidisciplinary approach to worship: our use of films, contemporary music, and readings from all spiritual traditions and cultures, as well as our direct engagement with each week's theme through a convergence of ritual and personal and community interaction. The fact that no two services are alike makes our approach to faith and worship both intriguing and refreshing.

We've also been featured in religious and spirituality-based magazines, newsletters, and journals. Though we have departed from the traditional church in many ways, most significantly in affirming seekers in their individual paths to God, our relationship to the traditional church and religion is not one of competition. By seeking publicity in religious publications, we're not trying to "steal" members away from the traditional church as much as we are trying to gain visibility and acceptance in the hope that church members who support our ministry will keep our community in mind when they become aware of seekers in their family and circle of friends.

There are, of course, many ways to spread the word about a new seeker community, and as we continue to grow, we will invent new approaches. We have not mentioned the necessity of patience and faith. In services we created to celebrate Journeys Community's first and second anniversaries, we used film clips from both *Witness* and *Field of Dreams*. In the drama *Witness* there is a scene in which an Amish community joins together to raise a barn in an afternoon. The scene exemplifies the hard work and sense of cooperation necessary to build a structure, and a community, together. *Field of Dreams*, of course, features the famous scene in which a farmer looks over his field of corn wondering if he should build a baseball diamond there. As he contemplates the craziness of his idea, the voice that comes to him says, "If you build it, they will come!" That famous line has been a source of sustaining faith for Harry and the ministry team at Journeys Community. We know that there are millions of spiritual seekers who have been unfulfilled by the traditional church; we believe that a seeker ministry designed specifically for seekers, affirming their individual paths and allowing them to worship the God of their own understanding, will allow many people the opportunity to connect with the Divine and with each other in a community of mutual respect.

CHAPTER 8

FILLING A SPIRITUAL NEED

Where does this seeker ministry lead? Church people would like our answer to be simply this: it leads to the church. They want to be reassured that our mission in forming a seeker ministry is legitimate and worthwhile; they expect a seeker ministry to funnel naturally into the traditional church, where previously "lost" people will come to be "found" in Christianity.

But when seekers ask us the same question, they are looking for a different answer because they're usually a bit suspicious about our motives. If it were the mission of Journeys Community to convert seekers, we would be failing as a seeker community. Even if seekers come to an understanding of God that is not much different from the traditional view, the fact is that seekers would rather ask their own questions and define their own beliefs. For us, Journeys Community leads to a deeper spiritual connection within ourselves, with the larger community, and with a personal God. Some fallen-away church people might be able to make peace with their religion and return to the church, as some members of Journeys Community have; some seekers might be inspired to consider traditional religion as part of their path; but the larger number of seekers continues with Journeys Community to celebrate and observe the transitions in their lives—birth, adulthood, marriage, illness, and death. Younger families may want a "Wee Journeys" program for children. As Journeys Community continues to grow, we'll add these components to our ministry, earning us additional credibility among seekers.

Some church members find it difficult to accept the real spiritual need for a seeker community as a legitimate way to know God. Recently, a member of Journeys Community shared this story with us: Michele was gathered with friends at her monthly book club meeting when one of her friends mentioned Journeys Community. She said to Michele, "I read an article the other day about that church you're involved with."

Michele, who prefers not to refer to Journeys Community as a "church" because of the negative associations the word evokes, said simply, "I call it a spiritual community; I don't think of it as church."

"No," said a third woman. "It is *not* church." This woman, a devout Baptist, had also read the article and disapproved of the concept behind Journeys Community. She didn't want to identify her idea of church with a "spiritual community." Her implication was this: because Journeys Community isn't an arm of an established religion and because it doesn't necessarily lead to a Christian understanding of God, it is less valid and authentic than church.

Michele smiled and kept her mouth shut. She knew there was nothing she could say that would change her friend's view. This is the kind of silence that seekers have kept for years; we've learned not to explain ourselves to church people because we know we will be misunderstood, our spiritual experiences oftentimes invalidated.

But that's why Journeys Community is so necessary. Instead of invalidating people's individual experiences of God, it helps to satisfy a genuine spiritual need as it encourages and celebrates this spiritual diversity and connection. It values people who don't fit into the conventional mold of belief and provides an atmosphere in which we can tangibly interact with the themes of our lives in a way that is personal, experiential, and deeply spiritual. Journeys Community helps to fill the deep spiritual longings of seekers for whom the destination is less important than the lifetime journey of looking for the Divine. Here are some stories and experiences that seekers have shared with us about how they've found fulfillment in our community.

Seekers Share Their Experience

Healing spiritual pain. It was at a quiet service titled "Contemplations on Faith" that a woman was reintroduced to thoughts about the importance of faith by ancient philosophers and mystics and early Christian contemplatives. It included spiritual readings written by Marcus Aurelius, Rumi, and one of the desert fathers, Hesychios. The readings were interspersed with silent meditations. After the service, the woman approached Harry and told him the service was exactly what she needed after the death of her sister. It touched her in a way that nothing else had and enabled her to get quiet enough to form her own approach to God in the midst of her grief and let the feelings pass through her.

Engaging spiritual experiences. "The first time I came to a Journeys Community service," says Jeff, "I was just amazed at the extent to which this group of people had thought through and created this wondrous experience to explore spirituality together in a way that is very well organized and yet very open and ecumenical and engaging."

Addressing pervasive violence in our society and in mainstream religion. Journeys member Larry wrote a moving email to the members of the ministry team to thank them for a service on nonviolence. The service was meant to enable people to look beyond the larger meaning of nonviolence in terms of war and abuse and recognize ways that we contribute to conflict in our daily lives. It centered on this question: how can we eliminate the passive violence that we are creating in our lives? As a multicultural service, it reflected on biblical verses focusing on Jesus' plea for us to love one another as well as our enemies; it also included quotes that typified Buddhist ideas about nonviolence, a Sufi's poem urging us to move beyond violence, and a passage written by Jewish scholar who devoted his life to conflict resolution and nonviolent communication. At a turning point in the service, members turned to bow and greet each other by saying, "Namasté," which translates, "The Divine in me recognizes and acknowledges the Divine in you." The service so moved Larry that he wrote this note:

> Passive violence really resonated with me this morning. Namasté is the opposite experience, a way to consciously remind me what to focus on. In my own life, it has been difficult for me to practice this with the woman I broke up with. I do not want to think of her, and when we meet, I have been keeping Namasté away, not wanting to see her as embodied with the Divine, not wanting to recognize and honor that. Not honor her. And this deliberate looking elsewhere on my part—that is passive violence. I am just now beginning to come to grapple with that. Today helped.

Overcoming misperceptions and long-held predjudices. A service titled "The Power of Words" had an important impact on another Journeys Community member. The service featured a rap song by Tupa Shakur, "Letter to My Unborn Son," and though the design team had wrestled with the idea of including a rap song in the service, unsure of how it would be received by the audience, they ultimately decided to include the song for its lyrics. After the service, a member approached someone on the ministry team and confessed, "Usually, I don't like that kind of music at all and feel nervous and threatened by it, but the words were so moving and heartfelt that I realized how much prejudice I carry with me. I would never have listened to that and considered it worthwhile on any other day. It made me reconsider the way I view people."

Finding spiritual truth in many cultures and faiths. The multicultural, multidenominational approach to our services allows seekers to transcend the dogma of religion and cultural prejudgments to get to the heart of a spiritual truth. This diversity is something that seekers appreciate week after week. "I like how the services cross all the boundaries of all the religions and takes the best of what they have to offer," Marcia explains. John likes the services because "it's like a church that doesn't have a religion; it just has spirituality. Nobody says anything that is against me. I like that. I feel comfortable here."

Recognizing the Divine in the experience of others. Not only does the design of the services enable us to go deep within ourselves and recognize the Spirit of God in our midst, but often we are greatly moved by listening to each other's life experiences of God. During an Easter service that focused on rebirth and renewal, one member shared in a group discussion about the rebirth she experienced after getting sober. She recounted the first spring when she had stopped drinking and how she saw a bed of tulips that amazed her. "It was as if I'd never seen tulips before and was seeing them for the first time in my life," she said. During the dark years of her life, she had never recognized how vivid and alive the world is. After experiencing such a profound transformation in her life, she was enthralled by the birds and the clouds and the flowers in spring. Though she has been sober many years, she said the experience reminded her that she needed to continue to look with fresh eyes at the world. After the service, several people shared with her their own experiences of darkness and depression; they felt a sense of comfort in knowing that they were not alone.

"People say things in these services that hit me in such a powerful way," remarks Paul.

"It is astounding," Chuck says. "There are many times when I've been brought to tears in a Journeys service." Others agree. Journeys Community offers seekers a voice that would be overlooked or dismissed in a traditional church. Not only do group discussions invite us to speak about our own spirituality in an atmosphere that is inclusive and accepting, but they allow many of us the chance to speak of spiritual things openly for the first time. Many people simply do not have this opportunity in the traditional church. The church leaves the teaching to the clergy and fails to recognize the wisdom of its members. But at Journeys Community, members often share intimate reflections about their lives. They have even helped design services with the ministry team as spiritual leaders looking to share their experience and hope. One Sunday, Evelyn acted as spiritual leader to speak on the theme, "Culture of Kindness" and the importance of practicing this spiritual tenet in daily life. Ken helped create another service titled "The Power of One" about the impact a single person can have on another person's life. Laura told her personal story of forgiveness and letting go at a service on healing. Patty led a powerful service, "The Language of Silence" that enabled us to become quiet and listen for the still, small voice within. Journeys Community has also invited outside speakers to share their unique perspectives with our community. For one Mother's Day service, Alison, a professional musician, spoke about the gift of music she received from her late mother. As a tribute, she played a Rachmaninoff concerto that had been particularly meaningful to both of them. Tatiana, a ceramic artist, joined Journeys Community for a service titled "Spiritual Expressions: The Energy of Artistic Intention," in which she described the spiritual and emotional teachings and personal meaning that went into the design of her ceramics. This shared wisdom enriches both the life of the speaker and the life of each community member and creates an intimacy that can't be replicated by the traditional church.

Experiencing variety in worship. Because each service is unique, there is a spirit of anticipation and excitement each Sunday morning as seekers arrive, and afterwards there is a feeling of gratitude. "Expect anything," Tom says. "That's why I love it so much." This sense of enthusiasm keeps seekers coming back to Journeys Community week after week. "It's always a surprise," says Allyson and her five-year-old daughter, Larisa.

Connecting with a caring community. In fact, when Janis and her husband, Jerry, were stranded in a hospital room in Arizona waiting for Jerry to recover from a sudden illness, they received a call from a member of Journeys Community on Sunday morning and were able to "attend" the service by listening by phone three thousand miles away—an example of how strongly attached seekers are to this community. "The thing I appreciate the most about being a part of Journeys," Janis explains, "is knowing that there is a group that I can feel very comfortable with and that I am a part of something larger than myself."

Every week, it seems someone is emotionally and spiritually moved by a service—either by a song or movie clip or reading or reflection, or the combination of them all—in a way that the design team never could have predicted or planned. We don't pretend to know exactly what people need to hear or experience each week to help them on their paths, but somehow these organic and authentic services are transforming people's lives by connecting them with a deeper Spirit.

Chuck explains it this way:

> It is the language of popular culture. Anything that is thematically engaging the culture as a whole becomes a viable pathway for meaningful communication with people who are seeking an experience of God but don't find religion to be accessible. . . . If we are able to engage more and more people and help them on their path toward God, then that godliness will benefit everyone. I truly do believe that Journeys Community could be as big a force for good in our culture as anything.

Joan, who is more practical in her explanation, says, "Everyone who comes says it touches them in such a deep place, and when they come in on Sunday morning, they feel so centered when they get here. For myself, Journeys services just carry me through the week and help me to be the kind of person that I want to be that sometimes I find it hard to be."

That people are so positively affected by our services is proof to us that the Spirit of God is guiding this seeker ministry. There have been too many spiritual coincidences in our services for us to assume all the credit.

At Journeys Community, all are invited to bring their hopes and longings, their desire to seek God both in the ordinary and in the extraordinary, and to share the fruits of their journey with others.

SAMPLE OUTLINES

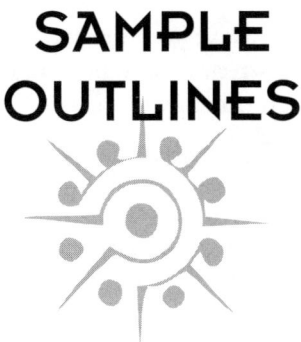

We've included three examples of the kind of services Journeys Community designs and hosts each week. These sample outlines for Journeys Community's services include comments that summarize the content we've used to develop these themes. We've included the services "Forgiveness," "How Is Prayer Expressed in Your Life?" and "Examen of Conscience: Meditations of St. Ignatius" to highlight the variety of spiritual content and experiences available weekly at Journeys Community. But it's impossible to fully represent the diversity of our services. Some of our services are centered around music to heighten the experiential nature of Journeys Community, while others are more symbolic in their spiritual convergence and meal. One of the services included as a sample allows for deep silence throughout the service. Others call for active participation from community members to engage the theme. Since every service is carefully organized to maximize the emotional depth of the theme and to heighten our connection with God, and since there's no prescribed pattern or order to our services, we've tried to explain, as much as possible, our intention for the direction and organization of each service.

Forgiveness

1. The Seating

As community members arrive for the service, thoughts about forgiveness are projected onto a screen at the front of the room. The quotes come from many sources and traditions. For example,

> Forgive, son; men are men; they needs must err.
> —EURIPIDES

> If we could read the secret history of our enemies, we would find in each person's life sorrow and suffering enough to disarm all hostility.
> —HENRY WADSWORTH LONGFELLOW

The quotes introduce the theme and offer a meditative atmosphere for community members as they enter the service.

2. Live Music

The musicians perform a rendition of the prayer of St. Francis as composed by Sarah McLachlan.[1] It is a meditative tune that expresses the humility of the prayer.

This song introduces the theme and expresses the essential idea that in forgiving others we receive forgiveness in return. The lyrics are projected onto the screen.

3. A Welcome

The spiritual leader welcomes community members to Journeys Community and introduces the theme that has already been set in motion with the quotes and the music.

4. A Reading

A member of the community reads a selected passage from the daily reader "One Day at a Time in Al-Anon." Part of the reading reminds us that if we judge another, we too are at fault and need to forgive ourselves. In forgiving ourselves we also forgive others.

The reading echoes the prayer of St. Francis and leads directly into the video clip which addresses this spiritual principle.

5. A Video

A clip from the movie *Dead Man Walking* is shown. The scene depicts a conversation between Sister Helen Prejean, played by Susan Sarandon, and the parents of a teenaged girl who was killed. In the movie, Sister Helen has decided to become the spiritual advisor of the killer and is confronted by the girl's parents, who lack sympathy and forgiveness for the "monster" who murdered their daughter.

This video is dramatic and stirring, illustrating the difficulty of forgivenss. It moves us into an emotional center in which we examine our own beliefs and limitations.

6. Live Music

The musicians perform the song "One" by U2,[2] which allows us to contemplate the ways we hurt and then forgive each other.

The lyrics are projected onto the screen. The song acts as a brief catharsis between the extreme emotions in the video clip and the reflection.

7. The Spiritual Reflection

The following discussion points for forgiveness are considered beforehand by the design team and the spiritual leader. They are incorporated into the spiritual reflection along with personal experience and stories to make the theme more accessible and engaging.

- Is there a difference between "large" forgiveness, as depicted in the video and in such atrocities as the Holocaust, and forgiveness on a smaller, everyday scale?
- How does forgiveness enter into our lives on a daily basis?
- Why is it hardest to forgive the people closest to us?
- Are there currently people in our lives whom we need to forgive?
- How can we forgive ourselves?
- How does the grace of God enter into our forgiveness?

8. A Meditation

A silent meditation follows the spiritual reflection for a period of five to eight minutes. The silence allows time for self-reflection and creates space for us to open our hearts to God and to others.

A calming image is projected onto the screen during the meditation.

9. A Recording

After the meditation, the community comes back together in conscious-ness to listen to a recording of "Broken Open: Suffering into Grace" by Wayne Muller.[3] A short segment of the recording tells the story of Cam-bodian refugees who were forced from their homes by Pol Pot. The refugees gathered to pray at a Buddhist ceremony and chanted, "Hatred never ceases by hatred, but by love alone is healed; this is an ancient and eternal law." In this way, the Cambodians sought to live a life of love and forgiveness toward their oppressors rather than live in anger and fear.

The recording brings the spirit of love into the service.

10. The Spiritual Convergence

At the front of the room is a punch bowl filled with water. It represents the "Common Bowl of Forgiveness" as described in the book *What's So Amazing About Grace* by Philip Yancey.

> The Benedictines . . . have a moving service of forgiveness and reconcilia-tion. After giving instruction from the Bible, the leaders ask each one attending to identify issues that require forgiveness. Worshipers then sub-merge their hands in a large bowl of water, "holding" the grievance in their cupped hands. As they pray for the grace to forgive, gradually their hands open to symbolically "release" the grievance.[4]

Community members are invited to come forward and enact the Benedictine ceremony.

The spiritual convergence is a physical manifestation of the willingness to forgive and has more transforming power than merely uttering the words, "I forgive."

11. The Spiritual Meal

The community is invited to come forward for a simple meal of bread as spiritual nourishment for our journey to forgive.

12. Live Music

The musicians perform "Let It Be" by the Beatles[5] to conclude the service.

The lyrics are projected onto the screen and the community is invited to sing along.

13. A Closing Prayer

The spiritual leader offers a closing prayer or some final remarks that summarize the theme of forgiveness.

How Is Prayer Expressed in Your Life?

1. The Seating

As community members arrive for the service, quotes about the nature of prayer and images of prayerful expressions from many religious traditions are projected onto a screen at the front of the room. For example, a photograph of a whirling dervish illustrates the idea that many forms of prayer are available to us.

The quotes and images introduce the theme and offer a meditative atmosphere for community members as they enter the service.

2. Live Music

The musicians perform "Hear Me, Lord," by Bonnie Raitt.[6] It is a lively tune that expresses our appeals to God.

This song was chosen as an introduction to represent the way in which most of us pray to God. The lyrics are projected onto the screen and the community is invited to sing along.

3. A Video

A video collage portrays various forms of prayer from around the world, such as Southern Baptist gospel singers performing, Catholic priests celebrating mass, Jewish boys reciting Hebrew prayers, Muslims bowing toward the east, Buddhist monks meditating, Hindus singing prayers, and Native Americans dancing. The edited video collage is taken from the movie *Baraka*.

This video underscores the theme by encouraging us to look beyond our preconceptions about prayer. It is a peaceful lead into the prayer that follows.

4. A Prayer and Meditation

The spiritual leader leads the community in a Native American prayer by White Eagle found in the collection *Worldwide Worship*, edited by John Marks Templeton. In part, the prayer reads:

> May thy peace and serenity bless us and the light of thy countenance shine upon our pathway henceforth and forever. In the silence may we feel the holy presence of God, our Creator. We open our hearts to the incoming of the light of God, praying that we may feel the impress of God's love drawing us all together in one spirit.[7]

This prayer leads directly into a moment of silence as the image of a single candle is projected onto the screen.

5. Live Music

The musicians perform a quiet song called "Peace" by Nora Jones.[8]
The lyrics are projected onto the screen. The melody of the song acts as an extended meditation.

6. A Reading

A member of the community reads a selected passage from the book *Praying with Our Hands* by Jon M. Sweeney. Part of the reading goes like this:

> We use our bodies to express ourselves in spiritual ways—and these physical expressions can be prayers too. For example, one way to show humility in God's presence is to prostrate oneself, or bow at the waist, or simply bow with the head. Are these expressions any less meaningful than a spoken prayer, such as "Lord, have mercy on me"?[9]

The reading leads directly into the spiritual reflection on this theme.

7. The Spiritual Reflection

The following discussion points for this theme are considered beforehand by the design team and the spiritual leader. They are incorporated into the spiritual reflection along with personal experience and stories to make the theme more accessible and engaging.

- Prayer is inviting the Spirit of God to enter us while letting go of our expectations.
- How do we open ourselves to God?
- How are listening, meditation, and contemplation forms of prayer?
- What have we learned about prayer in our lives?
- What are different ways that we can access our spiritual selves and connect with God?

8. The Spiritual Convergence and Meditation

As a community, participants are led in a spiritual chant. A member of the design team introduces the concept of chanting beforehand by referencing a text by Robert Gass, in which he explains:

> We chant to join our voices to the voices of countless seekers, worshipers, mystics, and lovers of life, in every time and in every place, who have shared in sacred song and to experience the communion that we feel with others when we come together in song. . . . Chants invoke the tangible

experience of Spirit and can be as informal as your family chanting the grace before meals. . . . Group chant also add a communal dimension to worship. . . . We pray together, we share our deepest selves.[10]

The community chants for several minutes before merging into a silent meditation.

The spiritual convergence is a tangible means of engaging participants with the theme and exploring alternative ways of worshiping God. The image of a single candle is projected onto the screen during the meditation.

9. The Spiritual Meal

The community is invited to come forward for spiritual nourishment. In keeping with the theme of many forms of prayer, participants are encouraged to take deep, cleansing breaths from bowls of fresh herbs (lavender, basil, rosemary, sage, and mint) to symbolically cleanse and renew the spiritual channel that connects them with God.

10. Live Music

The musicians perform "I Hear a Call" by Emmylou Harris[11] to conclude the service.

The lyrics are projected onto the screen and the community is invited to sing along.

11. A Closing Prayer

The spiritual leader offers a closing prayer or some final remarks that summarize the theme. Then community members are invited to stay for refreshments and fellowship.

Examen of Conscience: Meditations of St. Ignatius

1. The Seating

As community members arrive for the service, quotes are projected onto a screen at the front of the room while meditative music plays quietly. The quotes set the tone for the meditation to follow. For example:

> With an eye made quiet by the power of harmony, and the deep power of joy, we see into the life of things.
> —WILLIAM WORDSWORTH

The quotes and music offer a meditative atmosphere for community members as they enter the service.

2. A Reading

A member of the community reads a selected passage from *The Way We Pray* by Maggie Oman Shannon; the passage explains the purpose of an Examen of Conscience meditation. In part, it reads:

> The time-honored tradition of the Examen of Conscience (a period in which one reflects on the impulses expressed during that day) becomes not a self-flagellating confession of perceived misdeeds but a soulful search of one's own actions—and whether they have moved the individual closer to, or farther away from, God.[12]

The reading prepares the community for the deep meditation they're about to undertake during the course of the service.

3. A Spiritual Reflection

The spiritual leader welcomes the community and briefly explains the meditative format for St. Ignatius' Examen of Conscience. For this service the Examen is divided into five parts; each period of reflection is followed by silence and then music. The spiritual leader includes the following discussion points in his reflection on "Part 1: Prayer for Enlightenment."

- We recall we are in the presence of God and become sensitized to the loving presence of God in all of daily life.

- As we awaken our hearts to the love of God, we discover how often we are oblivious to God's love and grace, and how unconsciously we live.

- A regular examination of our conscience allows us to transform our hearts with the awareness of God's presence and love.

• The prayer for enlightenment reads in part: "May my understanding be always guided by you; may my heart be ever inflamed with love; may my will be ever conformed to your will, and may my whole life be a faithful following of you."

4. A Meditation

A silent meditation follows the reflection for a period of three minutes. The silence allows time to recall that we are in the presence of God and to contemplate the evidence of God in our daily lives.

An image of lighted candles is projected onto the screen as a point of focus during the meditation.

5. Live Music

The musicians perform "Every Grain of Sand" by Emmylou Harris.[13] It is a melodic piece about recognizing God in all aspects of our lives.

The lyrics are projected onto the screen. The song underscores the previous reflection and acts as a transition between the meditation and the next reflection.

6. A Second Spiritual Reflection

The spiritual leader briefly reflects upon the second aspect of the Examen and includes the following points while discussing "Part 2: Reflective Thanksgiving."

• We are dependent on God for everything, but when we gain means, affluence, skills, and positive feedback, we're likely to lose our accurate perspective and our humility.

• We must recognize our own poverty and our dependence on God, that we may become truly grateful.

• Let us meditate on this day's gifts, being concrete and specific and recognize our more permanent gifts of strength, ability to hope, humor, faith, family, and friends.

7. A Second Meditation

Another silent meditation follows for a period of three minutes. The silence allows time for community members to reflect upon gratitude and to give thanks to God for gifts received.

An image of lighted candles is projected onto the screen as a point of focus during the meditation.

8. Live Music

The musicians perform "Kind and Generous" by Natalie Merchant.[14] This is a popular, upbeat song about gratitude.

The lyrics are projected onto the screen. The song underscores the previous reflection and acts as a transition between the meditation and the next reflection.

9. A Third Spiritual Reflection

The spiritual leader continues the inward search of the Examen of Conscience by reflecting on "Part 3: Practical Survey of Actions."

- We must examine how we are living this day by reviewing our lives in detail.

- How is God communicating with us? In what areas of our lives is God especially calling for change?

- When we ask to receive God, we can see our actions and motives with honesty and patience.

- We ask God for the freedom to look upon ourselves without condemnation or complacency so we may be open to growth.

10. A Third Meditation

Another silent meditation follows for a period of five minutes. The silence allows time for reflection on how we can examine the way we are living our lives and ask God for the willingness to change.

An image of lighted candles is projected onto the screen as a point of focus during the meditation.

11. Live Music

The musicians perform the song "Penitent" by Suzanne Vega.[15] It is a reflective song asking for God's guidance.

The lyrics are projected onto the screen. The song underscores the previous reflection and acts as a transition between the meditation and the fourth reflection.

12. A Fourth Spiritual Reflection

The Examen of Conscience continues with the spiritual leader's brief reflection upon "Part 4: Contrition and Sorrow."

- We must confront our shortcomings and recognize their negative effects upon us.
- By understanding the impact of these negative behaviors, we can express our emotional response to them.

13. A Fourth Meditation

Another silent meditation follows for a period of five to seven minutes. The silence allows time for community members to respond emotionally to the inward reflection.

An image of lighted candles is projected onto the screen as a point of focus during the meditation.

14. A Fifth Spiritual Reflection

As the conclusion to the Examen of Conscience, the spiritual leader reflects on "Part 5: Hopeful Resolution for the Future."

- We look upon ourselves with compassion and recognize our need for God and see God's concern for us.
- After progressing through the steps of the Examen, we have a great desire to face the future with renewed vision and sensitivity.
- We allow hope to fill our hearts and pray, "I leave the past behind, and with hands outstretched to whatever lies ahead, I walk in the direction with renewed hope and peace."

15. A Final Meditation

A brief silent meditation follows for a period of two minutes. The silence allows time for hope to enter our hearts.

An image of lighted candles is projected onto the screen as a point of focus during the meditation.

16. The Spiritual Meal

The community is invited to come forward for a spiritual meal of "our daily bread," which symbolizes the basic sustenance we receive from God.

17. Live Music

The musicians perform "These Are the Days" by Van Morrison.[16] It is an upbeat song that expresses hope for the future.

The lyrics are projected onto the screen. This closing song punctuates the entire service.

18. A Closing Prayer

The spiritual leader ends the service with a prayer that reminds us to be thoughtful throughout the day. Then community members are invited to stay for refreshments and fellowship.

RESOURCE OF SERVICES

Included below is a list of themes from services we've designed and developed over the past four years. As a result of our weekly brainstorming and design sessions, we've amassed a library of spiritual material, including quotations, songs, prayers, images, readings, book suggestions, movie suggestions, and ideas for spiritual meals and convergences. If you would like to start a seeker community in your area or are interested in hosting a seeker service, our library of tested Journeys services is available to help you get started.

Acknowledging Fears

Agape

Aging and the Circle of Life

Amazing Grace

Anger

Anniversary

Ask Great Questions

Asking For Help

Authenticity

Beauty in Everything

Be Careful What You Say No To

The Beyond

Celebration of Life

Choosing Happiness

Christmas/Solstice

Compassion

The Connectedness of All Things

Connections: All Life Is Grass

Contemplations on Faith

Conversations with God

Creating Community

Creating Sacred Space

Creating Surprises

Creativity

NOTES

Preface

1. Bruce Bawer, *Stealing Jesus: How Fundamentalism Betrays Christianity* (New York: Three Rivers Press, 1997), 5.

Chapter 1: Wanderers Who Are Not Lost

1. Marcus J. Borg, *The Heart of Christianity: Rediscovering a Life of Faith* (San Francisco: HarperSanFrancisco, 2003), 210.

2. Tim LaHaye and Jerry B. Jenkins, *Glorious Appearing: The End of Days* (Carol Stream, Ill.: Tyndale House, 2004), 380.

3. Karen Armstrong, *The Battle for God* (New York: Ballantine, 2000), ix.

4. Bawer, *Stealing Jesus*, 11–12.

5. Neale Donald Walsch, *Conversations with God: An Uncommon Dialogue* (Charlottesville, Va.: Hampton Roads Publishing, 1997).

6. Wade Clark Roof, *A Generation of Seekers* (San Francisco: HarperSanFrancisco, 1993), 77–78.

7. Walter P. Kallestad, "Entertaining Evangelism," *The Lutheran*, May 23, 1990.

8. Jerry Adler, "In Search of the Spiritual," *Newsweek*, August 2005, 50.

Chapter 2: A New Spirituality—Journeys Community

1. *Thomas Berry: The Great Story*, VHS, produced by Nancy Stetson and Penny Morrell (2002).

2. Thomas Moore, *Care of the Soul: A Guide for Cultivating Depth and Sacredness in Everyday Life* (New York: HarperCollins, 1992), 4.

3. Adam D. Bradley, "The 'Emergent' Church," ZealForYourHouse.com, December 2004, http://www.zealforyourhouse.com/writeup.php/134.

4. Huston Smith, *The World's Religions: Our Greatest Wisdom Traditions* (San Francisco: HarperCollins, 1991), 209.

5. Tom Beaudoin, *Virtual Faith: The Irreverent Spiritual Quest of Generation X* (New York: Jossey-Bass, 1998).

6. Frederick Buechner, *Listening to Your Life* (New York: HarperCollins, 1992), 2.

7. *Thomas Berry.*

8. Richard Attenborough, comp., *The Words of Gandhi* (New York: Newmarket Press, 1996).

9. Rainer Maria Rilke, *Letters to a Young Poet* (trans. Stephen Mitchell; New York: Random House, 1984), 34.

10. Quoted in Jonathan Harvey, "Buddhism as a Bridge," *Unitarian Universalist Church of Palo Alto*, September 2002, http://www.uucpa.org.

11. Beaudoin, *Virtual Faith*, 176.

Chapter 4: Recruiting a Ministry Team

1. James Redfield, *The Celestine Prophesy* (New York: Warner Books, 1993).

Appendix 1: Sample Outlines

1. Sarah McLachlan, "Prayer of St. Francis," *Buffy the Vampire Slayer: Radio Sunnydale Soundtrack*, Virgin Records, 2003.

2. U2, "One," *U2: The Best of 1990–2000*, Universal Music International BV, 2002.

3. Wayne Muller, "Broken Open: Suffering into Grace" (Cassette; Louisville, CO: Sounds True, November 1994).

4. Philip Yancey, *What's So Amazing About Grace?* (Grand Rapids: Zondervan, 1997).

5. The Beatles, "Let It Be," *The Beatles: 1967–1970*, EMI Records Ltd., 1993.

6. Bonnie Raitt, "Hear Me, Lord," *Silver Lining*, Capitol Records, Inc., 2002.

7. John Marks Templeton, *Worldwide Worship: Prayers, Songs and Poetry* (Philadelphia: Templeton Foundation Press, 2000), 45.

8. Nora Jones, "Peace," *Don't Know Why*, EMI Int'l, 2002.

9. Jon M. Sweeney, *Praying with Our Hands: 21 Practices of Embodied Prayer from the World's Spiritual Traditions* (Woodstock, Vt.: Skylight Paths Publishing, 2000), 20.

10. Robert Gass and Kathleen A. Brehony, *Chanting: Discovering Spirit in Sound* (New York: Broadway Books, 1999), 10, 145–46.

11. Emmylou Harris, "I Hear a Call," *Cowgirl's Prayer*, Elektra Entertainment, 1993.

12. Maggie Oman Shannon, *The Way We Pray: Prayer Practices from Around the World* (Berkeley: Conari Press, 2001), 137.

13. Emmylou Harris, "Every Grain of Sand," *Wrecking Ball*, Elektra Entertainment Group, 1995.

14. Natalie Merchant, "Kind and Generous," *Ophelia*, Elektra Entertainment Group, 1998.

15. Suzanne Vega, "Penitent," *Songs in Red and Gray*, A&M Records, 2001.

16. Van Morrison, "These Are the Days," *Avalon Sunset*, Polydor/Pgd, 1989.

BIBLIOGRAPHY

Adler, Jerry. "In Search of the Spiritual." *Newsweek*, August 2005, 50.

Anderson, C. Alan. "Working Toward a Panentheistic New Thought." Paper presented at the Society for the Study of Metaphysical Religion, July 18, 1997. http://www.gis.net/~caa/work.html.

Armstrong, Karen. *The Battle for God*. New York: Ballantine, 2000.

Attenborough, Richard, comp. *The Words of Gandhi*. New York: Newmarket Press, 1996.

Bawer, Bruce. *Stealing Jesus: How Fundamentalism Betrays Christianity*. New York: Three Rivers Press, 1997.

Beatles, The. "Let It Be." *The Beatles: 1967–1970*. EMI Records Ltd., 1993.

Beaudoin, Tom. *Virtual Faith: The Irreverent Spiritual Quest of Generation X*. New York: Jossey-Bass, 1998.

Borg, Marcus J. "Spirituality and Contemporary Culture: Transcription from the 2000 TCPC National Forum." *The Center for Progressive Christianity*. http://www.tcpc.org/resources/articles/spirituality_and.htm.

———. *The Heart of Christianity: Rediscovering a Life of Faith*. San Francisco: HarperSanFrancisco, 2003.

Bradley, Adam D. "The 'Emergent' Church." ZealForYourHouse.com. December 2004. http://www.zealforyourhouse.com/writeup.php/134.

Brunett, Harry. "A Seeker Ministry for the Next Generation." Thesis, Seabury-Western Theological Seminary, 1998.

Buechner, Frederick. *Listening to Your Life*. New York: HarperCollins, 1992.

Eliot, T. S. *The Complete Poems and Plays: 1909–1950*. New York: Harcourt, 1952.

Gass, Robert, and Kathleen A. Brehony. *Chanting: Discovering Spirit in Sound*. New York: Broadway Books, 1999.

Harris, Emmylou. "Every Grain of Sand." *Wrecking Ball*. Elektra Entertainment Group, 1995.

———. "I Hear a Call." *Cowgirl's Prayer*. Elektra Entertainment, 1993.

Harvey, Jonathan. "Buddhism as a Bridge." Unitarian Universalist Church of Palo Alto, September 2002. http://www.uucpa.org.

Jones, Nora. "Peace." *Don't Know Why*. EMI Int'l, 2002.

Kallestad, Walter P. "Entertaining Evangelism." *The Lutheran*, May 23, 1990.

LaHaye, Tim, and Jerry B. Jenkins. *Glorious Appearing: The End of Days*. Carol Stream, Ill.: Tyndale House, 2004.

McLachlan, Sarah. "Prayer of St. Francis." *Buffy The Vampire Slayer: Radio Sunnydale Soundtrack*. Virgin Records, 2003.

Merchant, Natalie. "Kind and Generous." *Ophelia*. Elektra Entertainment Group, 1998.

Moore, Thomas. *Care of the Soul: A Guide for Cultivating Depth and Sacredness in Everyday Life*. New York: HarperCollins, 1992.

Morrison, Van. "These Are the Days." *Avalon Sunset*. Polydor/Pgd, 1989.

Muller, Wayne. "Broken Open: Suffering into Grace." Cassette; Louisville, CO: Sounds True, November 1994.

Raitt, Bonnie. "Hear Me, Lord." *Silver Lining*. Capitol Records, 2002.

Redfield, James. *The Celestine Prophesy*. New York: Warner Books, Inc., 1993.

Rilke, Rainer Maria. *Letters to a Young Poet*. Translated by Stephen Mitchell. New York: Random House, 1984.

Roof, Wade Clark. *A Generation of Seekers*. San Francisco: HarperSanFrancisco, 1993.

Shannon, Maggie Oman. *The Way We Pray: Prayer Practices from Around the World*. Berkeley: Conari Press, 2001.

Smith, Huston. *The World's Religions: Our Greatest Wisdom Traditions*. San Francisco: HarperCollins, 1991.

Sweeney, Jon M. *Praying with Our Hands: 21 Practices of Embodied Prayer from the World's Spiritual Traditions*. Woodstock, Vt.: Skylight Paths Publishing, 2000.

Templeton, John Marks. *Worldwide Worship: Prayers, Songs and Poetry*. Philadelphia: Templeton Foundation Press, 2000.

Thomas Berry: The Great Story. VHS. Produced by Nancy Stetson and Penny Morrell, 2002.

U2. "One." *U2: The Best of 1990–2000.* Universal Music International BV, 2002.

Vega, Suzanne. "Penitent." *Songs in Red and Gray.* A&M Records, 2001.

Walsch, Neale Donald. *Conversations with God: An Uncommon Dialogue.* Charlottesville, Va.: Hampton Roads Publishing, 1997.

Yancey, Philip. *What's So Amazing About Grace?* Grand Rapids: Zondervan, 1997.

CONTACT
JOURNEYS COMMUNITY

We are interested in hearing from you. Journeys Community is available to assist churches and other organizations that would like to develop their own seeker ministries. Our library of Journeys services is available to help you get a group started; we can also help you design your own individual seeker service based on the Journeys Community model. If you would like to find out more about Journeys Community or would like to host a service or start a seeker community in your area, please contact us:

Journeys Community
c/o Rev. Dr. Harry Brunett
5142 Durham Road W.
Columbia, MD 21044

Email: journeyscommunity@mris.com
www.journeyscommunity.org